THE
BIG BOOK
OF
FACTS, RECORDS
AND LISTS

D1392628

Also by Elizabeth Holt and Molly Perham
in Piccolo

Kids' London

THE
BIG BOOK
OF
FACTS, RECORDS
AND LISTS

compiled by
Elizabeth Holt

designed and illustrated by
Groom and Pickerill

A Piccolo Original

Piccolo Books

First published 1987 by Pan Books Ltd,
Cavaye Place, London SW10 9PG
© Elizabeth Holt 1986
Illustrations © Pan Books Ltd 1987
9 8 7 6 5 4 3 2
ISBN 0 330 29473 3
Photoset by Parker Typesetting Service, Leicester
Printed and bound in Great Britain by
Cox & Wyman Ltd, Reading

Contents

1 SPACE

The Universe

People used to believe that the Earth was the centre of the universe and that the Sun, the Moon and the stars revolved around it. It was a long time before they accepted the fact that, not only does the Earth revolve around the Sun, but it is also an insignificant part of the Milky Way – a galaxy consisting of more than 100,000 million stars – and our galaxy is only one of the millions whirling away in space.

Distance in Space

Distance in space is too vast for it is be expressed in kilometres. Instead, distances are measured by the time it takes light to travel to them.

Speed of light	=	300,000 km/sec
1 light year	=	9.5 million million km
1 parsec	=	3.26 light years

Journey	Distance
Sun—Earth	8 mins
Proxima Centauri (nearest star to Earth apart from Sun)—Earth	4.22 light years
Sirius (28 times brighter than the Sun)—Earth	8.7 light years
Sun—centre of The Milky Way	30,000 light years

Galaxies

Galaxies are huge clusters of stars and vary in size and shape. The majority are spiral in structure, either barred or with arms wrapped around them. Elliptical galaxies look rather like flattened balls. Others, known as irregulars, have no particular shape.

Apart from the Local Group, the galaxies closest to us, all the others appear to be moving away from each other, the most distant travelling at a greater speed than the rest. From this, it would appear that the universe is still expanding.

11

- The Small and the Large Magellanic Clouds, both irregular galaxies, are the closest to the Milky Way.
- Andromeda, a spiral galaxy similar to our own, can be seen from Earth as a distant smear on the horizon on winter evenings from the northern hemisphere.

Journey	Distance
Milky Way—Large and Small Magellanic Clouds	160,000 light years
Earth—Andromeda	2,120,000 light years

The Milky Way

Looked at from Earth on dark nights, the Milky Way appears to be a faint, rather hazy band of light in the sky. In fact, we are looking at the thickest part of our own galaxy. It is a spiral and rather like a discus since it is thinner at the edges than at the centre. Around its outer edge is a spherical halo consisting of old red stars and other clusters of stars.

The galaxy revolves around its own galactic centre, the stars within it revolving at different speeds.

Size	Distance
Diameter	100,000 light years
Maximum thickness	20,000 light years

The Solar System

The Sun is the hub of our solar system. Nine planets, including the Earth, together with their satellites and other bits of debris such as comets and asteroids, orbit it. The Sun's position in the Milky Way is about one third of the way from the perimeter to the central core.

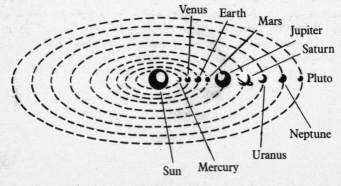

The Sun

Without the Sun we would not exist, for it provides the Earth with light and heat. Like all other stars, the Sun is different from the planets since it is a luminous ball of gas, whereas planets produce no light of their own and only shine because they reflect the Sun's light.

The Sun glows because it produces energy. This energy is the result of extreme pressure and incredibly high temperatures which produce nuclear-type explosions. During this process, 400 million tonnes of hydrogen fuse into helium every second and 4 million tonnes of matter are lost at the same rate. The Sun has become a yellow dwarf, half-way between the hottest and brightest stars and the coolest and dimmest. However, in spite of the fact that it consumes such vast quantities of hydrogen, it is estimated that the Sun still has a life span of about 10,000 million years.

Sun's Statistics

Mass	1.989×10^{27} tonnes
Density	1.407 (water = 1)
Size compared with the Solar System	99.866 per cent of all matter
Diameter	1,392,000 km
Time to rotate on axis	27 days (average)
Speed of rotation	7,050 km/h
Distance from Earth	150 million km
Inner core temperature	16 million°K

○ The *corona* is a thin gas which extends about 15 million km into space from the surface of the Sun with a temperature of about 1 million °C. It is clearly visible during a total eclipse.

○ *Flares* are violent storms that rage across the surface of the Sun.

○ *Prominences* are gigantic loops of gas that swirl out into space. The largest prominence recorded measured 588,000 km.

○ *Sunspots* are dark patches seen on the surface of the Sun. They are dark because they occur in areas where the temperature is lower, about 4,000°C. They vary in their extent. Some are several hundred kilometres across. The largest sunspot recorded covered an area of 18 million km^2.

13

Eclipse of the Sun

An eclipse of the Sun occurs when the Moon passes in front of it. If the Moon completely obliterates the Sun's light, it is called a total eclipse. If only part of the Sun is obscured by the Moon, it is called a partial eclipse. An eclipse has been known to last as long as 7 mins 31 secs.

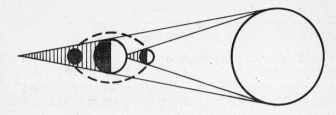

The Planets

Planet	Av. Distance from Sun (million km)	Approx Diameter km	Time to Orbit the Sun Yr	Day	Mass Compared to Earth
Mercury	58	4,880		88	0.055
Venus	108	12,300		225	0.815
Earth	150	12,756		365.25	1.000
Mars	228	6,790	1	321	0.107
Jupiter	778	142,800	11	315	318.000
Saturn	1,427	120,000	29	167	95.000
Uranus	2,870	50,000	84	6	14.520
Neptune	4,497	48,400	164	288	17.460
*Pluto	5,907	5,900	248	142	0.010

*So little is known about Pluto that estimates vary considerably.

Mercury

Mercury is the planet closest to the Sun. It lacks air and water but has a thin layer of gas around it. Its surface is rocky, and its lowland plains are probably covered by volcanic lava. With its numerous craters, probably caused by meteorites, it is not unlike the Moon in appearance.

Mercury's Statistics

Mass and gravity	1/20 that of Earth
Density	5.5 (water = 1)
Orbital velocity	48 km/sec
Temperature facing the Sun	400°C
Temperature on dark side of the Sun	−150°C
Surface gravity	0.38 (Earth = 1)

Venus

Venus, the second planet closest to the Sun, is similar to the Earth in size, but there the resemblance ends. It is concealed by a thick layer of unbroken cloud consisting of concentrated sulphuric acid. This reflects the Sun's light and makes it the brightest planet visible from Earth.

Venus's Statistics

Mass and gravity	4/5 that of Earth
Density	5.25 (water = 1)
Orbital velocity	35 km/sec
Temperature of outer clouds	−43°C
Temperature just below the clouds	330°C
Surface gravity	0.91 (Earth = 1)
Atmosphere	carbon dioxide 95%; minute amounts of carbon monoxide, water vapour, nitrogen, oxygen, hydrochloric and hydrofluoric acids and ammonias.

Note: Venus, unlike the other planets, rotates from east to west.

Earth

The Earth is not a complete sphere since it is flattened at the poles and has a south polar radius forty-five metres shorter than the north polar radius.

Earth's Statistics

Mass	$5,976 \times 10^{24}$ kg
Density	5.52 (water = 1)
Total surface area	510 million km^2
Land area	149 million km^2
Sea area	361 million km^2
Average height above sea level	857 km
Equatorial diameter	12,756 km
Polar diameter	12,714 km
Equatorial circumference	40,075 km
Volume	$1,083 \times 10^{21}$ m^3
Gravity acceleration	9.812 m/sec^{-2}

Earth's Satellite: The Moon

The Moon, which is over 4,700 million years old, is about a quarter of the size of the Earth. It has no air or water, and its illumination comes from the Sun.

It consists of solid rock and has rugged mountains and dark lowland plains. These plains, which are called seas, can be up to 1,000 km in diameter. Its surface is pitted with craters, probably caused by meteorites, but at one time there was almost certainly volcanic activity on it.

When the Moon is close to the Sun, it cannot be seen from Earth; but as it moves away, so more of it becomes visible. A new moon changing into a full moon, is said to be waxing; as it changes from a full moon back to a crescent, it is said to be waning.

Moon's Statistics

Mass	1/81 that of Earth
Density	3.34 (water = 1)
Diameter	3,476 km
Mean distance from Earth at nearest point	376,284 km
Time taken to orbit Earth	27 days, 7 hrs, 43.25 mins
Synodic period (time between new moons)	29 days, 12 hrs, 44 mins

Effect on tides *see*: The Earth, Weather

Mars

Mars is often called the red planet because of its colour. This is caused by the sands covering its desert areas, and the dust whipped into its atmosphere by the storms that whirl across its surface at speeds of up to 500 km/hr. The planet has polar ice caps, a gigantic rift valley 4,000 km long, and is volcanic, the largest volcano being 500 km wide and 20 km long.

Mars' Statistics

Mass	1/10 that of Earth
Mean relative density	3.94 (water = 1)
Diameter	6,786 km
Gravity	1/3 that of Earth
Distance from Earth at nearest point	56 million km
Temperature at equator	$-40°C$ (drops to $-70°C$ at night)
Surface gravity	0.38 (Earth = 1)
Atmosphere	mainly carbon dioxide; traces of carbon monoxide and water vapour

Mars' Satellites: Phobus and Deimos

Phobus and Deimos, are irregular shaped pieces of rock, the former 22 km and the latter 12 km across, orbiting Mars. It is thought that at one time they were asteroids which wandered too close to Mars and became attached to it by the force of its gravity.

Jupiter

Jupiter, the planet next to Mars, is a gigantic ball of hydrogen and helium which weighs 2.5 times as much as all the other planets in the solar system put together. Although composed of gases, it is possible that it has a small core of solid material in the centre. Jupiter is gradually diminishing in size since it is giving out 2.5 times as much heat as it receives from the Sun.

The multi-coloured bands which encircle the planet are actually clouds which have been whipped up by its rapid rotation.

Jupiter has a red spot, first observed in the 17th century. This is about three times the diameter of Earth, is oval shaped, and is thought by some people to be a permanently whirling cloud.

Jupiter's Statistics

Mass	318 times that of Earth
Density	1.33 (water = 1)
Surface gravity	2.64 (Earth = 1)
Equatorial diameter	142,984 km
Volume	1,321 times that of Earth
Atmosphere	methane, hydrogen, ammonia

Jupiter's Satellites

Jupiter has sixteen moons. The largest are Ganymede and Callisto, each of which is larger than Mercury. Their surfaces are similar with craters and patches of ice.

Saturn

Saturn is usually considered to be the most beautiful of the planets because of the bright rings around it. These are composed of millions of small pieces of rock coated in ice which have failed to coalesce into a satellite because they are too close to the planet. The diameter of the largest ring is about 272,000 km, but none of the rings is thought to be thicker than about 16 km.

Saturn's Statistics

Mass	95.14 times that of Earth
Density	0.71 (water = 1)
Surface temperature	−160°C
Surface gravity	1.16 (Earth = 1)
Atmosphere	hydrogen, ammonia, methane

Saturn's Satellites

Saturn has ten satellites, although it is believed that there might be as many as twenty-three. The largest is Titan, the only satellite with an atmosphere of its own, consisting mainly of methane.

Uranus

Because Uranus has an outer atmosphere consisting largely of methane, it appears greenish in colour. It consists of a rocky core with a thin layer of ice surrounding it, then there is a layer of liquid metallic hydrogen and one of liquid molecular hydrogen.

It differs from the other planets because its axis is tilted to such an extent that it rolls, rather than spins, through space. As a result, each pole is pointed away from the Sun for long periods so each has a winter lasting forty-two years. Uranus is encircled by rings of rocky debris, thought by some people to be the remains of an earlier satellite.

Uranus's Statistics

Mass	14.5 times that of Earth
Density	1.71 (water = 1)
Temperature	−200°C
Surface gravity	1.11 (Earth = 1)
Atmosphere	methane, hydrogen

Uranus's Satellites

Ariel, Miranda, Oberon, Titania and Umbriel are Uranus's five named satellites. However, several new moons were discovered orbiting Uranus during the 1986 Voyager 2 spacecraft flight. The total is now believed to be nearer fourteen.

Neptune

Neptune is the outermost of the giant planets and is thought to be similar to Uranus. It appears to be greenish in colour, and is thought to have a rocky core covered with ice.

Neptune's Statistics

Mass	17.2 times that of Earth
Density	1.77 (water = 1)
Temperature	−205°C
Surface gravity	1.21 (Earth = 1)
Atmosphere	methane, hydrogen

Neptune's Satellites

Neptune's two satellites are Triton and Neirid. Triton, believed to be the larger of the two, has a diameter of 6,000 km; about half that of Earth.

Pluto

Pluto, the smallest and faintest planet, is very distant, and was not discovered until 1930. It is thought to consist of a frozen ball of gas, and it has been suggested that at one time it was a satellite of Neptune. Pluto has an eccentric orbit so that between 1979–99 it will be closer to the Sun than Neptune and at its closest in 1989.

Pluto's Statistics

Mass	1/400 that of Earth
Density	4.5 (water = 1)
Temperature on sunlit side	$-214°C$
Surface gravity	0.43 (Earth = 1)
Average velocity	less than 5 km/sec

Constellations

Constellations are groups of fixed stars, usually named after mythological beings. The boundaries of eighty-eight constellations were fixed at a conference of the International Astronomical Association in 1930.

Some Important Constellations in the Northern Hemisphere

Scientific Name	Common Name
Andromeda	Chained Lady
Aquila	Eagle
Aries	Ram
Bootes	Herdsman
Cancer	Crab
Canis Minor	Smaller Dog
Cassiopeia	Mother of Andromeda
Cygnus	Swan
Gemini	Twins
Hercules	(Greek Hero)
Leo	Lion
Lyra	Lyre
Ophiuchus	Holding a Serpent
Pegasus	Winged Horse
Taurus	Bull
Ursa Major	Great Bear
Ursa Minor	Little Bear

Some Important Constellations in the Southern Hemisphere

Scientific Name	Common Name
Aquarius	Water Carrier
Canis Major	Greater Dog
Capricornicus	Goat
Centaurus	Monster (half man, half horse)
Corvus	Raven
Crater	Bowl or Jar
Eridanus	River Po (poetic name)
Hydra	Sea Serpent
Lepus	Hare
Libra	Scales
Lupus	Wolf
Sagittarius	Archer
Scorpius	Scorpion

Some Equatorial Constellations

Scientific Name	Common Name
Cetus	Whale
Orion	Hunter
Virgo	Virgin

○ Largest constellation   Hydra
○ Smallest constellation   Crux Australis

Stars

Stars are formed from huge clouds of dust and gas, and are composed mainly of hydrogen and helium in the ratio of 10:1, but they also contain heavier elements. It is thought that these heavier elements were originally part of the interiors of large stars which had exploded. If this theory is correct, young stars will contain more heavier elements than old stars.

Stars begin to form when the gases and dust are pulled together by the force of gravity. Then they begin to contract, until immense pressure and enormously high temperatures in their centres become so great that nuclear reactions take place. As this energy is produced, so the stars glow giving out both light and heat.

The colour of stars varies. Those that give out a bluish-white light are hotter than yellow ones like our Sun, and may have surface temperatures of up to 100,000°C. Red stars are cooler than yellow stars and may have surface temperatures of less than 2,000°C.

Magnitude

Magnitude is the unit of measurement for the brightness of fixed stars, the brightest being the lowest in the scale.

The Magnitude of Some Stars

Name	Magnitude
Sirius A	−1.46
Canopus	−0.73
Alpha Centauri	−0.29
Arcturus	−0.06
Vega	−0.06
Archernar	0.53
Algena	0.66
Acrux	0.87
Pollux	1.16
Beta Crucis	1.31
RG 0058.8–2807	20.20

Red Giant

A red giant is a star that is coming to the end of its life. As its reserves of hydrogen are used up, so it expands and becomes very bright until its outer layer of gas peels off and drifts away into space.

White Dwarf

A white dwarf is a red giant that has finally exhausted all its fuel. Once all of its outer layers have been shed, all that is left is a small, white, dense star. As it gradually cools, so it fades.

Supernova

This is a dying star which is at least five times the weight of our Sun. As it reaches the end of its life, it becomes a huge red giant, and collapses in a spectacular way becoming up to 10^8 times brighter as it erupts in a tremendous nuclear explosion.

Neutron Star

When a massive star is completely destroyed in a supernova, only a tiny core about 20 km in diameter will be left. It will be extremely dense and protons and electrons may fuse to give neutrons. This new star will rotate at a tremendous speed sending out energized particles in a highly directional beam.

Black Hole

If a really immense star collapses, it may turn into a black hole with a rim only a few kilometres in diameter. Its gravitational force will be so great that matter drawn towards it will plunge down the black hole and disappear from the known universe.

Some Astronomical Terms

Asteroids are bits of debris left over after the formation of the Solar System, or the remains of a planet that has disintegrated. The main asteroid belt lies between Mars and Jupiter. Although only about 200 asteroids are known, it is estimated that there may be more than 400,000, all with diameters of 1 km or more. Ceres, the largest, measures 995 km.

Aurorae is a display of luminous arcs, streamers and sheets of light, varying in colour, shape and intensity, seen in the sky in the regions of the poles. The auroras are caused by charged particles nearing the Earth where they are caught in its magnetic field.
   Aurorae Australis: southern polar lights
   Aurorae Borealis: northern polar lights

Comets consist of small particles of dust and debris with a nucleus thought to be composed of ice, and have a bright head and long tail. They travel in an elliptical or parabolic orbit around the Sun approaching it head-first, and leaving it tail-first. As they near the

Sun, they glow as they become warmer. Vaporization then takes place and the particles stream back and form the tail, which can be millions of kilometres long.

Halley's Comet, probably the best known, returns every seventy-six years. It last appeared in 1986 and was closest to the Sun on 1 February.

Eclipsing Binary Stars are two stars which are so close together that the force of gravity makes them orbit each other. At times, one of the stars is hidden behind the other resulting in an eclipse, and they appear much dimmer.

Algol consists of a dim yellow star and a smaller, but much brighter, blue star. Once every sixty-nine hours, the brightness of these stars decreases as the blue star is concealed by the yellow one.

Meteoroids and Meteorites are chunks of rock or metal which have probably broken away from asteroids or comets. These are meteoroids but on reaching the Earth's atmosphere they are called meteorites. Most burn up before reaching the surface of the Earth, but about 150 a year land on Earth and they vary in size from a few grammes to thousands of kilogrammes.

The largest meteorite found on Earth is near Grootfontein in South Africa. It is estimated to weigh 59 tonnes.

Meteoric Dust reaches the Earth's surface all of the time. It is estimated that up to 5 million tonnes arrive annually.

Pulsars are stars that act as a source of regularly fluctuating electromagnetic radiation. It is thought that they are neutron stars.

Red Shift is the displacement of the spectral lines emitted by a moving body. All galaxies move, and when the light emitted is towards the reddish end of the spectrum, the galaxy is receding. When the light emitted is at the blue end of the spectrum, it is approaching.

Solar Winds are streams of protons and neutrons. These are electrically charged particles emitted by the Sun, usually when there is sunspot activity or during solar flares, and they are sometimes trapped in the Earth's magnetic field forming the outer Van Allen radiation belt. Those that reach the upper atmosphere produce the auroral displays.

Exploration in Space

Although the space age really began in 1957, the first liquid-fuelled rocket, launched by an American, Robert H Goddard on 16 March 1926, travelled a distance of about 56 m and reached a height of 12.5 m.

Great advances in rocketry were made during the Second World War by the German scientist, Wernher von Braun, who continued his work in the USA once the war had ended. At the same time, scientists in the USSR were working on the exploration of space. Within eleven years of the end of the war with Germany, the world's first satellite was orbiting the Earth.

Sputnik 1

Launched	4 October 1957
Weight	83.6 kg
Diameter	58 cm
Velocity	28,565 km/h
Maximum altitude	946 km

Landmarks in Spaceflight

Country	Event	Date
USSR	first satellite Sputnik 1 in space	4 October 1957
USSR	Laika, a dog, first living creature in space in Sputnik 2	1957
USSR	Luna 2 crashes onto the Moon	1959
USSR	Luna 3 orbits the Moon and sends back pictures of its dark side	1959
USSR	Yuri Gagarin, first man in space in Vostok 1	12 April 1961
USA	John Glenn, first man to orbit the earth	1962
USA	Mariner 2 flies past Venus	1962
USA	Telstar, used for overseas TV communication launched	1962
USSR	Valentina Tereshkova, first woman in space in Vostok 6	16 June 1963

USSR	Aleksey Leonov, tethered to Voskhod 2, first man to walk in space	18 March 1965
USA	Surveyor 1 lands on the Moon and sends back pictures	1966
USA	first docking of a manned and unmanned spacecraft	1966
USA	first man to orbit the Moon in Apollo 8	1967
USSR	first docking of two spacecraft, cosmonauts from Soyus 4 transfer to Soyus 5	1969
USA	Neil Armstrong lands on the Moon with Edwin ('Buzz') Aldren	20 July 1969
USA/USSR	Spacecraft from each country dock together	1969
USSR	Luna 17, lands Lunokhod, a wheeled vehicle on the Moon	1970
USA	Mariner 9 orbits Mars	
USSR	Space capsule launched from Mars 3 lands on Mars	1971
USA	Skylab, first space workshop, put into orbit	1973
USA	Pioneer 10 passes through asteroid belt and flies past Mercury	1973
USA	Mariner 10 flies past Mercury	1974
USSR	Luna 24 sends a sealed container of rock samples from the Moon to Earth	1976
USA	Space Shuttle, with a design life of 500 space missions, launched	1981
USA	Bruce McCandless, first man to leave spacecraft and manoeuvre freely in space	1984
USSR	Svetlana Savitskaya, first woman to walk in space, who works on Salyut 7	25 July 1984
USSR	Vega spacecraft releases landing craft on to Venus	1985
USA	Voyager 2 expected to reach Uranus	1986
	Voyager 2 expected to reach Neptune	1989

2 EARTH

Earth, created from a whirling cloud of dust and gas that orbited the Sun at tremendous speed, is estimated to be about 4,600 million years old.

The Earth's Crust

Layers of the Earth

Name	Description
crust	the outer layer of the Earth; the continental crust generally averages 25 km thick but may be up to 50 km thick in some regions; the oceanic crust is up to 15 km thick

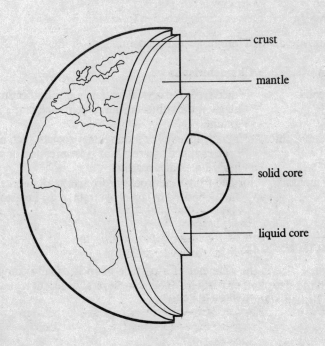

mantle	lies beneath the crust and consists of two layers separated by a transition zone; is up to 2,900 km in total thickness, the uppermost 50–200 km comprises the asthenosphere which is thought to be composed of molten or partially molten rock
core	the dense nickel-iron centre of the Earth, 6,800 km in diameter and with an estimated inner temperature of 4,500°C; the inner core has the properties of a solid and the outer core is probably liquid or semi-liquid

Plate Tectonics

The Earth's crust is a shell consisting of seven major and twelve smaller sections, or *plates*, which extend down to the upper mantle. These float on the molten magma of the mantle and are moved about by fairly sluggish thermal currents. This means that sometimes they are forced apart or squeezed together, occasionally resulting in volcanic activity or earthquakes.

Rocks

Rocks are divided into three main classes.

Name	Characteristics
igneous	formed from the crystallization and solidification of magma, the subterranean molten rock, e.g., granite
metamorphic	originally igneous or sedimentary rocks which have been changed as a result of great pressure or great heat, e.g., slate, marble
sedimentary	formed from other rocks or from organic sources and deposited in layers of strata, e.g., limestone, clay

Particle Size

Particle size is the diameter of a particle of rock usually compared with the size of other particles. There are several different scales, but the British Standard is widely used.

Class	Size (mm)
boulder	greater than 200
cobble	60–200
gravel	2–60
coarse sand	0.6–2.0
medium sand	0.2–0.6
fine sand	0.06–0.2
silt	0.002–0.06
clay	less than 0.002

Mountains, Mountaineering and Caves

The ten highest mountains are all in Asia.

The Top Ten Mountains

Name	Height (m)	Region
Everest	8,848	Nepal/Tibet
K2	8,611	Kashmir/Sinkiang
Kangchenjunga	8,586	Nepal/India
Makalu	8,475	Nepal/Tibet
Dhaulagiri	8,172	Nepal
Nanga Parbat	8,126	Kashmir
Annapurna	8,078	Nepal
Gashurbrum	8,068	Kashmir
Xixabangma Feng	8,013	Tibet
Nanda Devi	7,817	India

Some Other Mountains

Name	Height (m)	Region
Pik Kommunizma	7,495	USSR
Aconagua	7,014	Argentina
McKinley	6,194	USA
Logan	6,050	Canada
Kenya	5,200	Kenya
Ararat	5,165	Turkey
Mont Blanc	4,800	France

Name	Height (m)	Region
Matterhorn	4,477	Switzerland/Italy
Cook	3,764	New Zealand
Ben Nevis	1,343	Scotland
Snowdon	1,085	Wales
Carrantual	1,041	Ireland
Scafell Pike	978	England
Mount of Olives	617	Israel

Some Firsts in Mountaineering

Year	Mountain	Achievement
1776	Mont Blanc	J Balmat and M Paccard (France) reach summit
1808	Mont Blanc	M Paradis (France), first woman to reach summit
1861	Cameroun	Sir Richard Burton reaches summit
1865	Matterhorn	Edward Whymper and party reach summit
1871	Matterhorn	Lucy Walker (Britain), first woman to reach summit
1879	Kenya	Sir H Mackinder (Britain), C Ollier and J Brocherell (Switzerland) reach summit after hazardous month-long journey from Nairobi
1893	Cameroun	Mary Kingsley, Victorian woman explorer reaches summit
1897	Aconagua	M Zurbriggen (Switzerland) reaches summit
1934	Aconagua	dog (unnamed) reaches summit
1953	Everest	Edmund Hillary (New Zealand) and Tensing Norgay reach summit
1961	Mont Blanc	parachutists dropped onto summit
1975	Everest	Junko Tabei (Japanese), first woman to reach summit

Some of the World's Caves

Name	Depth (m)	Country
Reseau de Foillis	1,535	France
Snieznaja Piezcziera	1,479	USSR
Puerta de Illamina	1,338	Mexico
Sistema Huatla	1,246	Mexico

Name	Depth (m)	Country
Anou Ifflis	975	Algeria
Holloch	878	Switzerland
Ogof Ffynnon Ddu	309	Wales
Giant's Hole System	214	England
Reyfad Pot	179	Northern Ireland
Carrowmore Cavern	140	Irish Republic

Volcanoes and Earthquakes

Volcanoes

Volcanoes are classified as being active, dormant or extinct. Sometimes volcanoes which have been dormant for a very long time suddenly erupt, as did Mount St Helens in the USA, although it had not been active for over a century.

A further classification is based on the violence of the eruption. In increasing order of violence they are: Icelandic, Hawaiian, Strombolian, Vulvanian, Vesuvian and Peléan.

Areas of Major Volcanic Mountains

Region	Number
Japan and Formosa	64
Indonesian area	60
Central America	40
Kuril Islands (between Japan and USSR)	39
New Britain area (Papua New Guinea)	36
South America	34
Solomon Islands–New Zealand	33
Kamchatka (USSR)	25
Aleutian Islands	18
Alaska	15
Mexico	12
Philippines	12
USA (west)	3

The Top Ten Active Volcanoes (in order of height)

Height (m)	Volcano	Region
6,450	Antofalla	Argentina
6,060	Guallatìri	Argentina/Chile
5,897	Cotopaxi	Ecuador
5,320	Sangay	Ecuador
4,850	Kluchevskaya	USSR
4,269	Wrangell	Alaska
4,171	Mauna Loa	Hawaii
4,083	Galeras	Ecuador
4,070	Cameroun	Cameroon
3,959	Acatenango	Guatemala

The Top Ten Dormant Volcanoes

Height (m)	Volcano	Region
6,723	Llullaillaco	Argentina/Chile
5,777	Cayembe	Ecuador
5,670	Demavend	Iran
5,699	Citatépetl	Mexico
5,286	Ixtachuatl	Mexico
4,339	Cilima	Mexico
4,206	Haleakala	Hawaii
3,959	Acatenango	Guatemala
3,776	Juji-san	Japan

Top Ten Extinct Volcanoes

Height (m)	Volcano	Region
6,960	Aconagua	Argentina
6,885	Ojos de Salados	Chile
6,550	Tupungato	Argentina
6,267	Chimborazo	Ecuador
5,633	El'brus	USSR
5,452	Popocatepetl	Mexico
5,199	Kenya	Kenya
4,764	Cumba	Ecuador
4,720	Ruminahu	Ecuador
4,506	Karisimbi	Zaire

Some Shattering Volcanic Eruptions

Year (AD)	Event
79	Vesuvius, Italy, exploded. The town of Pompeii, together with most of its inhabitants, was buried beneath a thick layer of ashes. Herculaneum, a town on the other side of the volcano, was also buried. The steam that accompanied the ash made it set like concrete
130	Taupo, New Zealand, erupted. $16,000\,km^2$ of the surrounding area was flattened. It has been estimated that 30,000 million tonnes of pumice was ejected
1815	Tambora on Sumbawa, an Indonesian island, erupted resulting in the death of about 90,000 people, many of them from the ensuing famine. The height of the island was lowered by 1,250 m, and the resulting crater had a diameter of 11 km
1883	Krakatoa, a small volcanic island in the Sunda Strait, exploded. Dust and clouds reached a height of 28 km and the following explosions were heard over 4,775 km away. Two thirds of the island was destroyed, a huge tidal wave killed over 40,000 people and more than 160 villages were obliterated
1956	Bezmianny, in the Kuril Islands, erupted ejecting $2.8\,km^3$ of matter and hurling particles of dust 45 km in the air. It took three days before volcanic dust reached this country. 185 m was sliced off the top of the mountain
1985	Nevada del Ruiz, Colombia, erupted. The heat from the volcano melted snow and ice and a huge river of mud flowed down into the valley below, burying the town of Armero and killing 23,000 people.

Some Other Facts About Volcanoes

o The largest volcanic crater in the world is that of Toba in north-central Sumatra. Its area is $1,775\,km^2$.

o In 1783 Laki, in Iceland, erupted. Its lava flow was about 65 km long. In 1947 Laki ejected $1\,km^3$ of material.

o Geysers are steam/water spouts found in volcanic areas. The geysers in Waimangu in New Zealand, which are no longer active, shot boiling water, stones and mud up to a height of 450 m.

Earthquakes

When an earthquake takes place, the crust moves and the earth itself quivers. If the tectonic plates are forced against each other, this will cause stress and if this becomes too great, the plates will shift and split. This results in shock waves which might start as deep as 700 km beneath the surface of the Earth. The epicentre of an earthquake is the place on the surface that the shock waves first reach.

Seismic zones are narrow, well-defined belts where the majority of earthquakes occur. The Circum-Pacific belt is an area where seventy-five per cent of present earthquakes take place.

There are various ways of measuring earthquakes. The Richter scale compares their magnitude, but the Modified Mercalli Scale is the one that people understand most readily.

Modified Mercalli Scale

Scale **Effect**

I shock felt by few people

II shock felt mainly by people indoors and resting, especially on upper floors of buildings; some suspended objects, such as lamps, swing about

III shock noticeable indoors; stationary cars may rock slightly

IV shock very noticeable indoors; people asleep woken up; doors and windows rattle

V noticeable out of doors; cracking noises of walls indoors; objects fall; pendulum clocks might stop

VI everyone feels shock and many are frightened; some slight structural damage to buildings; heavy furniture moves or is overturned

VII frightened people rush into the street; slight damage to reasonably constructed buildings; rather more damage to those in bad condition

VIII considerable alarm; substantial damage to poorly built buildings; chimneys, factory stacks, monuments collapse

IX poorly built buildings collapse; others moved from their foundations; ground cracks and underground services badly damaged, pipes broken

X panic; destruction of all but the best-constructed buildings which are themselves damaged; bigger ground fissures; rails bent; landslides at river banks

| XI | most buildings completely destroyed; fissures widen; bridges destroyed; underground services distintegrate; landslips in soft ground |
| XII | destruction almost total; waves seen on the surface of the earth; land deformed |

Some Shattering Earthquakes

Year (AD)	Event
1556	greatest loss of life due to earthquake ever when an estimated 830,000 people were killed in Shensi, Honan and Shansi provinces of China
1906	The San Francisco earthquake in the USA devastated about $10.5 \, km^2$, destroyed 28,000 houses, 34 schools and scores of other buildings. Much of the damage was due to the subsequent fire, though only about 700 people were killed
1970	The mountain in Peru, Callejon de Huaylas, had its northern peak ripped away and a huge mass of rock and debris shot down the mountainside gathering even more debris. It split into three prongs and engulfed the whole region. About 70,000 people died, 50,000 were injured, and over 186,000 buildings were destroyed. The calamity was triggered by a violent earthquake in the Pacific fifteen miles from the Peruvian coast causing tremendous shock waves inland
1985	Mexico City, the most densely populated urban area in the world, was devastated by an earthquake registering 8.1 on the Richter scale. It (too) began out in the Pacific with shock waves travelling toward the city at 25,000 km/h. More than 9,000 people died in the centre of the city, 30,000 were injured and 95,000 left homeless. The cost of reconstruction has been estimated at more than four billion dollars.

Some Other Facts About Earthquakes

○ Japan's greatest earthquake was in 1923. Over 142,500 people were killed, many in the resulting fires; in Tokyo and Yokohama alone 575,000 buildings were destroyed.

○ In 1977 there was earthquake in Tangshan, China. Although the original death toll announced was much higher, the official figure now is 750,000.

Islands and Deserts

Islands

Islands are areas of land surrounded by water which are not continental land masses.

The Top Ten Islands

Island	Region	Area (km²)
Kalaatdlit (Greenland)	North Atlantic	2,130,265
New Guinea	South-West Pacific	794,090
Borneo	South-West Pacific	751,078
Madagascar	Indian Ocean	589,683
Baffin Island	Canadian Arctic	476,066
Sumatra	Indian Ocean	431,892
Great Britain	North Atlantic	229,522
Honshu	North-West Pacific	226,087
Ellesmere	Canadian Arctic	198,393
Victoria Island	Canadian Arctic	192,695

Some Other Islands

Largest freshwater: Ilha de Marajo, Amazon, Brazil
Largest lake island: Mantouline, Lake Huron, Canada
Most recent: Lateiki, resulting from a volcanic eruption; annexed by Tonga (South Pacific) in 1979.

The Top Ten Deserts

Deserts are generally agreed to be arid areas of land where there is less than 250 mm mean annual rainfall.

Desert	Location	Area (km²)
Sahara	North Africa	8,400,000
Gobi	Mongolia	1,295,000
Gibson	Western Australia	647,500
Great Victoria	Western and Southern Australia	647,500
Rub al Khali	Southern Arabia	587,500

Desert	Location	Area (km²)
Kalahari	Southern Africa	562,500
Taklamakan	China	450,000
Great Sandy	Western Australia	375,000
Nubian	Northern Sudan	375,000
Atacama	Northern China	350,000

Oceans and Seas

The oceans were formed from the clouds of steam that enveloped the Earth when the planet was still immensely hot. The Earth gradually cooled and, in time, the steam turned to rain which fell back to Earth. Pools of water turned into lakes and the lakes became seas. Eventually, the seas joined up to become one ocean surrounding one land mass called Panagea.

In time, Panagea split into two. Gondwanaland consisted of Africa, Antarctica, Australia, India and South America. Laurasia consisted of Asia, excluding India, and Europe and North America. Slowly, these continents drifted apart until they formed the land masses, seas and oceans of today.

Statistics

Area of Earth covered by sea	361,000,000 km²
Percentage of Earth covered by sea	70.92%
Volume of oceans	1,285,600,000 km³
Deepest part of ocean: Marianas Trench in the Pacific	10,915 m
Highest submarine mountain: near Tonga Trench between New Zealand and Samoa	8,690 m from sea bed
Lowest temperature: White Sea	−2°C
Highest temperature: Persian Gulf in summer	35.6°C

The Top Ten Oceans and Seas

Name	Area (km^2)
Pacific Ocean	165,384,000
Atlantic Ocean	82,217,000
Indian Ocean	73,481,000
Arctic Ocean	14,056,000
Mediterranean Sea	2,505,000
South China Sea	2,318,000
Bering Sea	2,269,000
Caribbean Sea	1,943,000
Gulf of Mexico	1,544,000
Sea of Okhotsk	1,528,000

Some Other Seas

Name	Area (km^2)
East China Sea	1,248,000
Yellow Sea	1,243,000
Hudson Bay	1,233,000
Sea of Japan	1,008,000
North Sea	575,000
Black Sea	461,000
Red Sea	438,000
Baltic Sea	422,000

Tides

Tides are the regular rising and falling of the seas and oceans, and are the result of the Sun and the Moon's gravitational pull on the Earth, but the effect of the Moon is roughly twice that of the Sun. The normal interval between tides is 12 hrs 25 mins.

Tide	Effect
ebb	the receding, or falling, tide following high tide and preceding low tide
flood	the incoming of the tidal stream preceding high water

Tide	Effect
neap	occurs when the gravitational pull of the Sun is at right angles to that of the Moon; the high tides are lower than usual, the low tides higher; neap tides occur twice a month when the Moon is in the first or the third quarter
spring	occurs when the Earth, the Sun and the Moon are in a straight line so that the Sun is pulling in the same direction as the Moon; the high tides are higher than usual, the low tides lower; spring tides occur twice a month around the time of the new Moon and the full Moon

Lakes, Rivers, Canals and Waterfalls

Lakes

Lakes are enclosed areas of water, usually, but not always, fresh water, which the sea cannot enter. The areas of lakes vary considerably. Lake Chad, once one of the world's great lakes, is now very much smaller than it was five years ago.

The Top Ten Lakes

Lake	Location	Area (km^2)
Caspian Sea (salt)	USSR–Iran	360,700
Superior	Canada–USA	82,350
Victoria	Kenya–Uganda–Tanzania	69,410
Aral (salt)	USSR	66,000
Huron	Canada–USA	60,700
Michigan	USA	58,000
Tanganyika	Tanzania–Zambia–Zaire–Burundi	32,900
Great Bear	Canada	31,800
Baikal	USSR	31,600
Great Slave	Canada	28,450

Some Other Lakes

Lake	Location	Area (km^2)
Maracaibo	Venezuela	16,300
Titicata	Peru–Bolivia	8,340
Gairdner	Australia	7,770
Torrens (salt)	Australia	5,780
Lough Corrib	Ireland	168
Loch Lomond	Scotland	70
Windermere	England	26

Rivers

Rivers are streams of water flowing in a channel from high ground to low ground and into a sea or a lake, although in desert areas they may simply disappear. Claims are made that the Amazon is longer than the Nile, but that is only true if the River Pará is considered a tributary of the Amazon.

The Top Ten Rivers

River	Location	Length (km)
Nile	Africa	6,695
Amazon	South America	6,570
Mississippi/Missouri	North America	6,020
Yangtze	Asia	5,530
Ob/Irtysh	Asia	5,410
Huang He (Yellow)	Asia	4,840
Zaire (Congo)	Africa	4,630
Paraná	South America	4,500
Irtysh	Asia	4,440
Amur	Asia	4,416

Some Other Rivers

River	Location	Length (km)
Mackenzie	USA	4,240
Volga	USSR	3,688
Indus	Pakistan–India	3,180
Rhine	Germany	1,320

River	Location	Length (km)
Seine	France	761
Shannon	Ireland	386
Severn	Wales–England	354
Thames	England	346
Tay	Scotland	188
Usk	Wales	104

Canals

The remains of an irrigation canal constructed c.5000 BC have been found in Iraq, and it is thought that canals were dug even earlier in China. One section of the Grand Canal in China was completed c.4000 BC and several sections were linked together in about AD 600.

Some Canals, Canal Systems and Artificial Seaways

Canal	Location	Length (km)	Opened
Volga–Baltic Canal System	USSR	2,300	1965
St Lawrence Seaway	Canada	304	1959
Beloye More Baltic Canal	USSR	227	1933
Suez Canal	Egypt	162	1869
Kiel Canal	Germany	98	1895
Panama Canal	Panama	92	1914
Manchester Ship Canal	UK	57	1894
Terneuzan-Ghent Canal	Netherlands/ Belgium	29.5	1895
Nieuwe Waterweg	Netherlands	27	1872
North Sea Canal	Netherlands	23.5	1876
Corinth Canal	Greece	6.5	1893

Waterfalls

Waterfalls occur in rivers where the water descends vertically. Over a long period of time a waterfall will move upstream as the lip of fall becomes eroded.

The Top Ten Waterfalls
(by drop from lip to base)

Fall	Country	Height (m)
Angel Falls	Venezuela	979
Ribbon Fall	USA	487
Upper Yosemite	USA	430 (total fall 491)
Garvenie	Pyrenees	428
Wollomombi	Australia	335 (total fall 518)
Staubbach	Switzerland	298
Seward	Peru	270
Vetifoss	Norway	261
King Edward VII	Guyana	256
Gersoppa	India	253 (total fall 276)

Some Other Waterfalls

Name	Height (m)	Width (m)
Khone (Laos)	21	10,800
Niagara (Canada)	49	793
(USA)	54	330
Victoria (Zimbabwe, Zambia)	122	1,700

Atmosphere and Weather

The Atmosphere

The atmosphere is a thin layer of tasteless, colourless and odourless gases surrounding the earth, and it is divided into concentric layers according to the rate of temperature change with height. The tropopause, stratopause and mesopause separate the layers.

Composition of the Atmosphere

nitrogen	78.09%
oxygen	20.95%
argon	0.93%
	99.97%

The remaining 0.03 per cent consists of carbon dioxide and very small amounts of hydrogen, helium, krypton, methane, neon, ozone, xenon and water vapour.

Concentric Layers of the Atmosphere

Layer	Elevation Above Earth's Surface	Characteristics
Troposphere	up to 10 km	contains practically all the water vapour and 75% of total gaseous mass; temperature decreases with height at a mean rate of 6.5°C/km
Tropopause Stratosphere	10–50 km	contains the greater part of the atmospheric ozone but very little water vapour; temperatures in the upper zone increase with height between 20 km and 50 km; winds can be quite strong
Stratopause Mesosphere	50–80 km	temperature decreases from 0°C to −50°C at the mesopause
Mesopause Thermosphere/ Ionosphere	80+ km	temperature increases with height; the ionosphere is sometimes considered as extending from 100 km–300 km; because of frequent disturbances caused by geomagnetic storms and sunspot activity, radio communications can be upset

Van Allen Belts

Two belts discovered by J Van Allen in 1958 in which ionized particles are concentrated, having been trapped by the Earth's magnetic field. The bands are at heights of 3,000 km and 16,000 km above the Earth's surface. It is believed that the outer belt contains particles originating from the Sun.

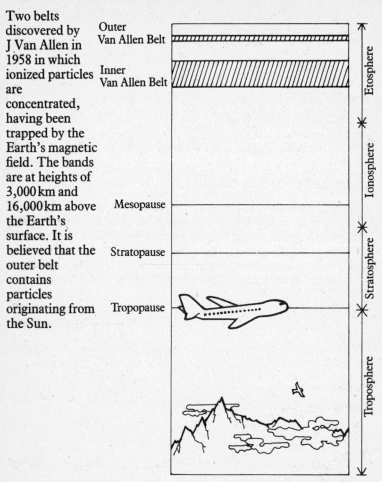

Weather

Weather is the state of the atmosphere at a specific time in a specific place. It has to take into account atmospheric pressure, humidity and wind, but other factors are also involved.

Measurement of Atmospheric Pressure

Atmospheric pressure is the pressure exerted on the surface of the earth by the weight of the atmosphere, and it is measured in millibars.

1,000 millibars = 1 bar = 10^5 pascals

Atmosphere	Millibars
Average pressure (sea level)	1,013.25
Highest recorded (Siberia, USSR)	1,083
Lowest recorded (Pacific, west of Guam)	870

Humidity

Humidity is the measurement of the amount of water vapour in the air. It can be calculated or measured in various ways, and it is frequently expressed as relative humidity. The higher the humidity, the greater the discomfort. There is a comfort index which assumes that people feel at their best when there is a relative humidity of 40–70% and an air temperature of 15.5°C–27°C.

Country	Max–Min Relative Humidity (%)
Bahrain	89–39
Mauritania	91–26
Oman	94–20
Somalia (Mogadishu)	81–57
United Arab Emirates (Ras Al-Khaimah)	100–24

Precipitation

This is water deposited on the earth in the form of snow, sleet, hail, rain, drizzle and dew.

Snow

Snow is a solid form of precipitation consisting of snowflakes and tiny spicules of ice. Ice spicules form when the temperature is well below freezing point but, as the temperature rises, they become snowflakes.

Amount of Snow	Equivalent Water (mm)
300 mm newly fallen snow	25
100–150 mm wet compact snow	25
500–700 mm dry powdery snow	25

Snowline

The snowline is the limit on high ground which represents the lower limit of perpetual snow. The altitude of the snowline varies according to the region in which it occurs.

Snowline (m)	Region
5,000–6,000	tropics
2,500–2,700	Alps, Pyrenees
1,200–1,400	Northern Scandinavia
600	Southern Kalaatdlit (Greenland)
sea level	high polar latitudes

Ice

Ice is the solid state of water. It takes many forms on the surface, including black ice, hail, rime and glaciers. An iceberg is a mass of ice in the sea exceeding 5 m in height. An ice-floe is any area of sea ice measuring at least 20 m across.

Hail

Hail is composed of pellets of ice, usually 5–50 mm in diameter. The largest recorded hailstone had a diameter of 190 mm, a circumference of 444 mm, and weighed 750 g.

Sleet

Sleet is a mixture of rain and snow, or partially melted falling snow.

Rain

Rain is composed of separate drops of water formed by the condensation of water vapour in the atmosphere and falling from clouds to the Earth's surface. The intensity of rainfall is measured by dividing the total rainfall measured in mm by the number of rainfall hours.

Intensity	mm/hr
heavy rain	greater than 4
moderate rain	0.5–4
light rain	less than 0.5

Some Facts About Rainfall

○ The most intense rainfall was experienced in Barst, Guadeloupe in 1970 when 38.1 mm was recorded in one minute.

○ Kauai, Hawaii has had as many as 350 rainy days in one year.

○ Wisbech, Cambridgeshire, experienced 51 mm of intense rainfall in 1970 in 12 minutes.

Wind

Wind is the horizontal movement of air caused by variations of pressure as a result of the differential heating of the Earth's surface. The direction of wind can be indicated by a weather-vane which consists of a vertical spindle with a pivoted horizontal arm. The arm has a broad surface, or tail, at one end so that wind pressure swings the opposite end in the direction from which the wind is blowing.

Wind velocity is measured on the Beaufort Scale. This scale, ranging from 0–12, was devised by Admiral Sir Francis Beaufort in 1806 to indicate the strength of winds. It was modified later by the US Weather Bureau which added the numbers 13–17.

Force	Velocity (mph)	Description	Characteristics on Land
0	0–1	calm	smoke rises vertically
1	1–3	light air	smoke slowly drifts
2	4–7	light breeze	leaves rustle; weather-vane moves
3	8–12	gentle breeze	wind on face; leaves and twigs in constant motion
4	13–18	moderate breeze	small branches in motion; dust and litter blown about
5	19–24	fresh breeze	small trees sway; wavelets on inland water

Force	Velocity (mph)	Description	Characteristics on Land
6	25–31	strong breeze	large branches sway
7	32–38	near gale	whole trees in motion; walking difficult
8	39–46	gale	twigs break from trees; walking very difficult
9	47–54	strong gale	branches break; some slight structural damage to buildings, e.g., tiles fall
10	55–63	storm	trees uprooted; severe damage to buildings
11	64–72	violent storm	widespread damage (rarely experienced inland)
12	73–82		
13	83–92		
14	93–103	hurricane	creates havoc, loss of life; mainly in the tropics, rarely inland
15	104–114		
16	115–125		
17	125–136		

Clouds

Clouds are visible masses of minute droplets of water or ice crystals. They exist at sea level in the form of fog or mist, and reach a height of about 13,700 m. The classification of clouds is based on appearance and height. They are divided into low, middle and high clouds, but cumulus, cumulonimbus and nimbostratus do not always fit into these categories.

Low Clouds

Cloud	Altitude (m)	Characteristics
stratus 	up to 500	grey, uniform base, thin sheets; after 500 m becomes another stratiform cloud; often turns to drizzle
cumulonimbus	may reach 10,000	dark grey or black; huge dense vertical masses resembling cauliflowers with a more fibrous flattened top spreading out like an anvil; indicates thunderstorms, hail or snow
cumulus	460–2,000	white or greyish; horizontal base, upper parts dome-shaped; also white puffy balls; sometimes indicates fine weather but when cauliflower-shaped and approaching cumulonimbus in size, may bring heavy rain, hail or snow
nimbostratus	900–3,000	dark grey; in thick sheets so Sun not visible; often indicates rain or snow

49

Cloud	Altitude (m)	Characteristics
stratocumulus	500–2,000	whitish or grey; extensive horizontal layers in globular masses, usually without a break, but sometimes dark areas separated by small areas of clear sky or thinner cloud

Middle Clouds

Cloud	Altitude (m)	Characteristics
altocumulus	2,000–7,000	white or grey; patches or layers of thin, globular clouds often separated by blue sky
altostratus	2,000–7,000	greyish; continuous thin sheet or veil of uniform appearance with Sun visible through thinner parts of cloud; frequently followed by rain

High Clouds

Cloud	Altitude (m)	Characteristics
cirrocumulus	5,000–13,700	white; thin, rippling layers or sheets with a mottled appearance, often called a mackerel sky
cirrus	5,000–13,700	white; wispy strands; when extra long strands are whipped out by strong winds in the upper atmosphere, they are called mares' tails; often indicates rain
cirrostratus	5,000–13,700	milky white; smooth transparent sheets which produce a halo effect around the Sun; indicates an approaching depression

Some Other Clouds

banner	stationary clouds that seem to be attached to an isolated mountain peak; the name comes from the fact that the cloud extends downwind resembling a banner
noctilucent	clouds in the high atmosphere observed at ground level when it is getting dark; sometimes bluish-white or yellow, occasionally brilliant; height about 80 km

Storms

Storms are violent atmospheric disturbances characterized by strong winds and usually accompanied by rain, snow, hail, sleet or dust.

lightning	a visible flash of light in the sky caused by the discharge of atmospheric electricity from one cloud to another or from a cloud to the Earth; the flash travels at 0.1 times the speed of light, and transmits a current of 10,000 amps; sheet lightning is thought to be the reflection of lightning flashes which the observer is unable to see
thunder	the result of the rapid heating and expansion of the air by the flash of lightning, thus causing sound waves; the speed of sound is not as great as the speed of light, so the thunder follows the flash of lightning. Distance from the flash can be roughly measured by assuming 1.6 km for each 5 second interval between the flash and the rumble

Rainbows

Rainbows are caused by the refraction and internal reflection of sunlight through falling raindrops or spray, but can only be seen if your back is to the sun. The bigger the raindrops, the brighter the colours.

Colours of the Rainbow

Red
Orange
Yellow
Green
Blue
Indigo
Violet

fogbows	are similar to rainbows but can only be seen in a fog with your back to the sun. They are arcs of brighter light but are colourless since the droplets are too small for refraction and reflection to create colours
double rainbows	are formed when some of the light falling onto the raindrops is reflected twice. The secondary or outer bow is less distinct and its colours are reversed

Some Other Geographical Terms

Cold pole is the location in each hemisphere where the lowest air temperatures have been recorded. In the northern hemisphere this is Verkojansk and Oimjakon in Siberia ($-68°C$). In the southern hemisphere this is Vostok on the Antarctica Ice Plateau ($-88.3°C$).

Equator is the imaginary circle lying midway between the poles and is formed at the surface of the Earth by a plane drawn through the centre, perpendicular to its axis; the longest circumference of the Earth.

Latitude is the angular distance of a point on the surface of the Earth, north or south of the equator, as measured from the centre of the Earth. Latitude is measured in degrees, minutes and seconds.

Longitude is the angular distance measured along the equator between the meridian through a given point. Since 1884 the meridian through the Old Royal Observatory at Greenwich has been the prime meridian, so longitude is measured from 0°–180° east or west of Greenwich.

Tropic of Cancer is the parallel of latitude roughly 23.5°N indicating the extreme northern positions at which the Sun appears directly overhead at noon.

Tropic of Capricorn is the parallel of latitude roughly 23.5°S indicating the extreme southern positions at which the Sun appears directly overhead at noon.

Rain Day is a period of 24 hours commencing from 0900 GMT on which a minimum of 0.2 mm of rainfall is recorded.

Wet Day is a period of 24 hours commencing from 0900 GMT on which a minimum of 1.00 mm of rainfall is recorded.

3 THE LIVING WORLD

At first there was no life on Earth. The environment was hostile. It was too hot and its atmosphere too poisonous for life to develop; but gradually conditions changed. As the Earth cooled and the oceans were formed, so the atmosphere changed too. The sea and the air possessed the chemicals from which living organisms are made, and energy came from the Sun and other sources. This permitted the chemicals to link themselves together as molecules of protein able to reproduce themselves. So life began; but it took millions of years before man inhabited the Earth.

Evolution

Evolution is a process of gradual, but continuous change by which a species develops from its original state to its state today. This means that all plants and animals have developed from earlier ones. Birds, for instance, have developed from dinosaurs, dinosaurs from reptiles, reptiles from amphibians, and amphibians from fish. Some species were unable to adapt to a changing environment and became extinct.

Some Extinct Animals

Name	Characteristics	Million Years Ago
Meganeura mony	(Europe) huge dragonfly, wing span up to 70 cm	280
Labyrinthodont	(Antarctica) freshwater amphibian, not unlike a salamander	200
Stegosaurus	(Northern Europe) armoured dinosaur with plates 1 m wide; up to 9 m long; up to 1.75 tonnes in weight; brain about 70 g	150

Name	Characteristics	Million Years Ago
Diplodocus	(Northwest America) plant-eating dinosaur; long neck and tail; length up to 25 m	150
Deinosuchus riograndensis	(Western America) crocodile, up to 16 m long	75
Tyrannosaurus Rex	(Midwest America) flesh-eating dinosaur; height up to 5.5 m; length up to 12 m	75
Quetzalcoatlus	(Western America) large flying creature with wing span up to 12 m	65
Gigantophis	(Egypt) snake up to 11 m long	55
Carcharodon	great shark up to 13.1 m long	15
Dromornis stirtoni	(Australia) huge flightless bird up to 3 m high, not unlike an emu	11
Geochelone atlas	(Asia) huge tortoise up to 2.4 m long; up to 850 kg in weight	2
Dinornithes	(New Zealand) moa, huge wingless bird between 0.6 m and 3.6 m high with strong limbs and long neck	1.5

Fossils

Fossils are the traces or preserved remains of plants and animals that existed long ago. Since rocks are found in layers, or strata, and the lowest strata is the oldest, it is possible to work out when the plant or animal existed from the layer of rock in which it is found.

Geological Time Chart

Period	Development	Million Years Ago
Pre-Cambrian	immense volcanic activity; formation of igneous rocks, deposits of iron ore; development of algae and sponges	2,000

Period	Development	Million Years Ago
Cambrian	sedimentary rocks by end of period; marine invertebrates	570
Ordovician	volcanic activity, seas flood and recede, deposits of zinc and limestone; molluscs and first corals	480
Silurian	mudstone and limestone; leafless land plants; fishes with jaws, earliest vertebrates	440
Devonian	coniferous trees; lobe-finned fishes, primitive amphibians, spiders and scorpions	395
Carboniferous	shallow seas, deltaic sandstones and shales with coal seams from forests; fish, amphibians develop, primitive reptiles	345
Permian	reptiles and modern insects such as beetles and cicadas develop	280
Triassic	red sandstone; reptiles dominant, first dinosaurs appear	225
Jurassic	clays and limestones, coral reefs; dinosaurs dominant, flying reptiles, Archeopteryx (the first bird) and mammals appear	195

Period	Development	Million Years Ago
Cretaceous	flowering plants, bony fish, many reptiles and dinosaurs become extinct	135
Eocene and Oliocene	Alps fold; mammals abundant, dominance of higher mammals, modern carnivores, bats and whales, tortoises and turtles	65
Miocene	grasses appear and spread; pigs, primates, horses, rhinoceroses, elephants	26
Pliocene	development of marine life; primates develop and spread; early man appears in Africa	7
Pleistocene	extremes of temperature; glaciers advance and recede in the northern hemisphere; man develops	1.5

Classification of the Animal World

Since all animals have developed from an earlier species, and many are related to each other, they have been classified in groups in an order which begins with the simplest and ends with the most complex.

Phylums

A phylum is a group of animals with a common basic structure. It is divided into subphylums, and subphylums are divided into classes. Classes are split into orders, orders into families, and families into the genus and species. A European wolf, for instance, is *Canis lupus*, and a domestic dog is *Canis familiaris*.

Classification of the Domestic Dog

Phylum	Cordata
Subphylum	Verbrata
Class	Mammalia
Order	Carnivora
Genus	*Canis*
Species	*Canis familiaris*

Phylum	Subphylum	Characteristics
Protozoa		single-celled organisms, mostly only visible under a microscope; over 80,000 described; e.g., amoeba
Coelenterata		multicellular with nerve cells; hollow bodies with two layers of cells separated by a layer of jelly; e.g., sea anemones, jellyfish
Platyhelminthes		three layers of cells; worm-like with a nervous system, some with an alimentary system; e.g., tapeworms, flatworms
Mollusca		soft, unsegmented bodies, usually partially or wholly enclosed in a shell, with a foot or sticky pad,

Phylum	Subphylum	Characteristics
		gills and a mantle; e.g., oysters, snails, squids
Arthropoda		jointed legs; segmented body usually divided into head, thorax and abdomen; well-developed nervous system, eyes and antennae
	Arachnida	four pairs of legs; lung-like sacs or breathing tubes; body divided into two sections; e.g., spiders, mites, scorpions

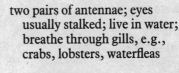

	Crustaceans	two pairs of antennae; eyes usually stalked; live in water; breathe through gills, e.g., crabs, lobsters, waterfleas

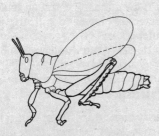

	Insects	head with antennae; three pairs of legs; three pairs of jaws; broadly divided into those with wings and those without; e.g., butterflies, beetles, locusts, fleas

- The arthropods are the largest phylum (80% of all animal species).
- There are approximately 850,000 named species of insects.
- The largest insect in the world is *Goliathus giganteus*, the Goliath beetle, found in equatorial Africa and weighing up to 100 g.
- The largest order of insects is the Coleoptera with about 275,000 named species of beetles and weevils.
- It is estimated that there are about 500,000 million spiders in the UK.

Phylum	Subphylum	Characteristics
Chordata		includes animals with a notochord – a gristly rod that supports the backbone or vertebrae; vertebrates have a skeleton made of bone or cartilage, a spinal chord protected by a backbone, a well-developed nervous system and a brain protected by a skull
	Fish	waterproof, streamlined bodies with fins and gills; the pectoral fins steer and balance the body, those at the end of the tail are used for thrust; fish can be divided very generally into those with bony skeletons and those made of cartilage

- *Rhincodon typus*, the whale shark, is the biggest fish in the world and weighs up to 43 tonnes.
- One of the most dangerous fish is the piranha. It is similar to a carp and has razor-sharp teeth. If a wounded person or an animal falls into a river, a shoal is attracted by blood and will strip all the flesh from the body within minutes.
- *Electrophorus electricus*, the electric eel, often discharges 400 volts at one ampere.

Phylum	Subphylum	Characteristics
Chordata	Amphibians	live partly on land, partly in water; must return to water to breed; most must live in moist conditions; e.g., frogs, toads

- The largest amphibian in the world is the Chinese *Andrias davidianus*, a salamander weighing up to 65 kg and 18.5 m in length.
- The commonest toad is *Bufo marinus*, the marine toad, which is found throughout the world.

Phylum	Subphylum	Characteristics
Chordata	Reptilia	cold-blooded vertebrates which slither or crawl, some with short, stubby legs; Chelonians, such as tortoises and terrapins, have protective shells so that only heads, legs and tails protrude

o The world's largest reptile is *Crocodylus porosus*, the salt-water crocodile, which can weigh up to 2 tonnes.
o *Python reticulatus*, the reticulated python, found in south-east Asia, is the longest snake and can reach 10 m in length.
o The largest lizard is the Komodo monitor. This reptile, looking rather like a dragon, can weigh up to 59 kg.
o The South American *Eunectes murinus*, the anaconda, is the world's heaviest snake and may weigh over 225 kg.

Phylum	Subphylum	Characteristics
Chordata	Aves	includes all birds; warm-blooded, have feathers and light, strong skeletons with a ridge down the breastbone to which the muscles needed for flying are attached; sight is excellent, and hearing keen; flightless birds such as kiwis and cassowaries do not have a ridged breastbone

Some Facts About Birds

o There are about 100,000 million birds in the world.
o There are nearly 9,000 species, over half of them passerines, or perching birds, such as sparrows, thrushes and starlings.
o There are over 300 species of birds of prey such as owls, kestrels and eagles.

○ The fastest bird in level flight is *Hirundapas caudacutus*, the white-throated spine-tailed swift, which can reach a speed of over 170 km/h.
○ The largest bird is the ostrich which may weigh over 155 kg and be up to 2.7 m tall.

Beaks

A bird's beak is formed of hard epidermal coverings over the upper and lower jaws, and a pair of nostrils, sometimes fringed with bristles. The beak, which renews itself as old cells are replaced by new, is used for grooming and nest-building, but its main purpose is to acquire and grip food, so its shape is related to the diet of the bird.

Shape of Bill	Type of Food
small, slender	insectivorous; the prey can be picked up singly or, as in the case of swallows and swifts which feed on the wing, gathered into widely gaping beaks
strong, chisel-like	insectivorous; the bird is capable of boring holes into the bark of trees to reach the insects it feeds on; e.g., woodpeckers
hook-tipped, often sharp edged	carnivorous; able to kill prey and rip up flesh; e.g., owls, hawks
short, stout, strong	seed-eaters; able to crack and remove husks from seeds; e.g., sparrows, finches
long, dagger-like, serrated edges	fish-eaters; the saw edge enables the bird to grasp slippery edges
long bill, sometimes broad and flat	filter food from water; e.g., flamingoes, geese

Eagle   Goose   Curlew   Heron

Herring Gull   Puffin   Finch   Woodpecker

Feet

Usually a bird has four toes, but the shape and arrangement of them are adapted to its way of life.

Type of Bird	Type of Feet
perching birds	three toes in front, one powerful toe behind
climbing birds	most have two yoke-shaped in front, two others behind
birds of prey	three toes in front, one behind; wide grasp and powerful hooked talons
walking birds	three toes in front, one behind; short blunt claws
wading birds	three elongated toes in front, one behind giving support on soft or marshy ground
swimming birds	three toes in front, one behind; webbed feet acting like paddles
running birds	many have only three toes on each foot; the ostrich has only two

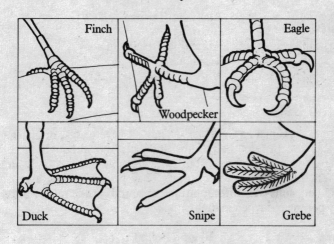

Finch

Woodpecker

Eagle

Duck

Snipe

Grebe

Phylum	Subphylum	Characteristics
Chordata	Mammalia	warm-blooded, a complete diaphragm, heart with four cavities, fleshy lips, a well-developed brain and nervous system, teeth set in sockets. In most cases the young are born alive and suckled by their mothers. The only flying mammals are bats

Some Marsupials

Marsupialia are pouch-bearing mammals. The female posseses an abdominal pouch into which the newly-born baby climbs. Inside the pouch is a nipple which the baby clings to with its mouth. However, the baby is not capable of sucking the milk and so the powerful muscle of the nipple squirts it into its mouth.

Name	Region Found
Kangaroo	Australia, Tasmania, New Guinea
Koala	Australia
Short-tailed opossum	Argentina, Brazil, Guiana
Tasmanian devil	Tasmania
Virginian opossum	USA (south and east), Argentina

Some Bats

Bats are classified as *Chiroptera*. They all have wings, or alar membranes, attached to their limbs and tails and although these are different from the wings of birds, they enable the bats to fly almost as well. Most bats are nocturnal. They find their way about and avoid collisions by emitting ultrasonic sounds at the rate of thirty to sixty per second when in flight.

Name	Region Found
Great vampire bat	Mexico, Paraguay
Horsehoe bats	Asia, North Africa, Europe (southern and central)
Indian flying fox	Burma, Ceylon, India
Little brown bat	North America
Long-tongued fruit bat	Africa, Australia, India, New Guinea

Gestation and Incubation

Gestation is the period of time the young is carried, from its conception to its birth. Incubation is the time taken for an egg to hatch.

Animal	Gestation (Days)	Average no. in Litter	Maximum Life Span (Years)
antelope	215–275	1–2	20
ass	375	1	45
badger	180	3–5	15
brown bear	210–250	1–2	31
camel	350–400	1	40
cat (domestic)	60	3–6	20
chimpanzee	270	1	50
elephant, African	640	1	70
fox	54	3–8	14
giraffe	440	1	28
hare	42	2–5	10
hippopotomus	240	1	41
horse	325	1–2	60
human	270–280	1	120
kangaroo	40	1	13
lion	106	2–4	40
mouse	21	4–8	4
orang-utan	260	1	50
pig	115	6–20	15
porpoise	360	1	15
rhinoceros	560	1	40
sheep	150	1	14
whale, blue	330	1	30
zebra	375	1	30

Bird	Incubation (days)	No. of Eggs	Colour of Eggs
albatross, royal	77–80	1–2	white
blackbird	15	4–5	greenish
corncrake	15	6–14	grey with brown spots
falcon, peregrine	30	3–4	white with brown spots
flamingo, greater	32	2	chalky white
goose, greylag	28	3–7	whitish

Bird	Incubation (days)	No. of Eggs	Colour of Eggs
jackdaw	18	4–6	greenish with brown spots
lark	12	3–4	yellowish with brown spots
mallard	26	7–14	greenish
nightingale	14	4–5	brownish-green
oystercatcher	27	2–4	light brown with dark spots
puffin, common	42	1–2	white, frequently spotted
owl, barn	32	2–4	white
owl, long-eared	28	4–5	white
thrush, song	14	4–5	greenish-white
vulture, griffon	51	1	brown with red spots

Primates

Primates, the most highly developed order of mammals, includes monkeys, apes, and promisians such as tree shrews and bushbabies, as well as man.

Primates	Characteristics
monkeys	basically four-footed but able to sit upright and use 'hands', skull more rounded than those of other mammals; live in trees; mainly vegetarian.
	New World monkeys are flat-nosed and live in trees. Some have a long prehensile tail which can be wrapped around branches so that all four limbs are free.
	Old World monkeys live on the ground, have well-developed noses, and their tails (if they have them) are non-prehensile. Baboons and mandrills, the largest of this group, have big teeth and long muzzles.

Primates	Characteristics
anthropoid apes	man-like with a highly developed brain, tailless, large jaws and teeth; mainly vegetarian. The group includes chimpanzees, considered the most intelligent of the apes; orang-utans with long arms, reddish hair and a pouch beneath the chin; gorillas with black skin and hair and very long arms; and gibbons, which live mainly in trees and use their long arms to swing from branch to branch.

Man

The Skeleton

The skeleton, which is made up of 206 bones, is the body's supporting framework. It also protects vital organs as well as providing something for the muscles to attach themselves to.

It is composed of two materials, bone and cartilage. When an embryo is formed, its skeleton consists entirely of cartilage, but by the time the baby is born, most of this has been replaced by bone.

Some Bones in the Skeleton

Name	Function
clavicle	small bone connecting the sternum with the shoulder blade
femur	thighbone extending from the pelvis to the knee; the longest bone in the body
fibula	long, thin outer bone of the leg extending from the knee to the ankle
humerus	bone in the upper arm extending from the shoulder to the elbow
patella	knee cap
pelvis	ring of bone formed by the ilium, the ischium pubis and the sacrum, and supporting the spinal column

radius	shorter and thicker of the two bones of the forearm on the same side as the thumb, extending from the elbow to the wrist
ribs	12 pairs of arched bones attached to the backbone and enclosing the chest cavity; consists of 7 pairs attached to the sternum (true ribs), 3 pairs attached to the lower of the true ribs (false ribs), and 2 pairs unattached in front (floating ribs)
scapula	two flat, triangular bones in the back of the shoulder and attached to the humerus
tibia	inner and thicker of the two bones of the leg extending from the knee to the ankle
vertebrae	33 short bones forming the spinal column with 7 verticle (for the neck muscles), 12 thoracic (for connection to the ribs), 5 lumbar (for the back muscles), 5 sacral (for attachment to the pelvis), 4 fused together to form the coccyx, man's vestige of a tail
ulna	the larger of the two bones of the forearm on the side opposite the thumb and extending from the elbow to the wrist

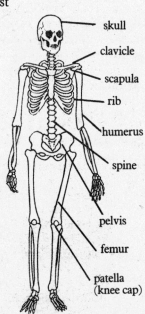

skull

clavicle

scapula

rib

humerus

spine

pelvis

femur

patella
(knee cap)

The Skull and the Brain

The skull is the bony framework of the head and it protects the brain, eyes and ears. It consists of bones fused together, and is hinged to the lower jaw.

The brain controls all of the body's activities. Different parts have different functions.

Name	Description
medulla	at the very top of the backbone where nerves entering the skull are massed; controls unconscious activities such as breathing and digestion
cerebellum	above the medulla; coordinates muscular activity
cerebrum	grey matter, the largest part of the brain, concerned with intelligence, speech, memory, learning, and so on; divided into two hemispheres, the left controlling the right side of the body, the right controlling the left

Unlike other cells, once the cells of the brain are damaged or die, they are not replaced. Although the brain is well protected and is suspended in liquid, any damage to it can affect mental and physical abilities, and personality.

Teeth

Teeth first appear when a baby is five to eight months old, and by the time the child is about two years old, it will have a complete first set of twenty. These are pushed out as thirty-two permanent teeth (sixteen in each jaw) appear.

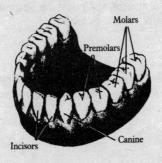

Molars

Premolars

Incisors

Canine

69

Name	Function
incisors	two wedge-shaped cutting teeth on each side of the jaw
canine	one on each side of the jaw; used for grinding and chewing (sometimes called dog, or eye teeth)
premolars	two on each side of the jaw; used for chewing and grinding
molars	three on each side of the jaw; used for chewing and grinding

Eyes

All primates have two eyes, and each gives a slightly different picture of the object it is looking at. The eye consists of several main parts.

Name	Function
schlera	the white outer part of the eye; attached to a protective socket by three muscles which allow the eye to move; also protected by the eyelid and by fat
choroid	an inner layer containing blood vessels supplying the inner part of the eye; prevents blurred vision as light is reflected in the eye
retina	layer beneath the choroid with light-sensitive cells; rods respond to dim or dark light and give black and white vision; cones respond to bright light and give colour vision
cornea	bends light rays so that they fall onto the retina
lens	focuses light by contracting or relaxing muscles
iris	the coloured part of the eye in front of the lens controlling the size of the pupil
pupil	the central part of the iris through which light passes; if light is strong, the pupil becomes smaller; if it is weak, the pupil becomes wider

Tears

Everyone produces tears all of the time. They are secreted from ducts behind the top eyelid and their job is to wash away dust and other irritants.

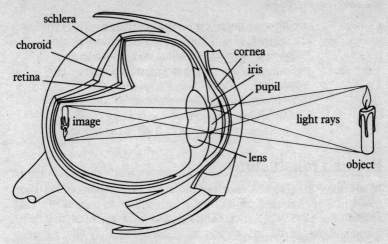

The diagram shows labels: schlera, choroid, retina, image, cornea, iris, pupil, light rays, lens, object.

Common Eye Defects

Astigmatism occurs when the shape of the cornea is deformed so that horizontal and vertical lines cannot be seen clearly at the same time. This is corrected by the use of a cylindrical lens.

Hypermetropia is the condition of being long-sighted where the eyeball is shorter than normal. The rays of light are focused behind the retina so that distant objects are seen more clearly than near ones. This is corrected by the use of a converging lens.

Myopia is the condition of being short-sighted where the eyeball is longer than normal. Light rays from distant objects are focused in front of the retina so that the objects are not seen distinctly. This is corrected by the use of a diverging lens.

Blood

There are four major blood groups, A, B, AB and O. Each may have chemicals called antigens, A and B, on the surface of the red blood cells, and each may have chemicals called antibodies, anti-A and anti-B, in the plasma.

Blood Group	Type
A	contains antigen A on the red blood cells and antibody anti-B in the plasma
B	contains antigen B on the red blood cells and antibody anti-A in the plasma
AB	contains antigens A and B on the red blood cells and no antibodies in the plasma
O	contains no antigens on the red blood cells and antibody anti-A and anti-B in the plasma

Blood Transfusions

If you have an accident and lose more than forty per cent of your blood in a very short period of time, you will be in danger of dying unless you have a blood transfusion; but it is essential that your blood and that of the donor's is compatible so that they mix.

Blood Group	Receives Blood from	Gives Blood to
A	A and O	A and AB
B	B and O	B and AB
AB	all groups	AB only
O	O only	all groups

Some Facts About the Body

o There are about 700 million air sacs, called alveoli, in the body.
o The digestive tract, called the alimentary canal, is about 10 m long and it can take food up to 24 hours to pass through it.
o The body has about 6.2 litres of blood; 1 mm^3 has about 4.5 million red blood cells and 700 white blood cells; it takes about a minute for blood to go from the heart, around the body, and back again.
o An adult brain weighs about 1.5 kg.
o An adult male's heart beats about 70 times a minute; the size of an animal determines the number of heartbeats (a bird's heart beats about 500 times a minute).
o Muscles account for about two-fifths of the body's weight.
o Skin, the body's waterproof outer covering, is about 1 mm thick and has two layers: the epidermis, the thin outer layer; and the dermis, the thicker lower layer; fingertips do not have an outer layer and that is why they have ridges, whirls and loops.

○ The normal temperature of the body is 27°C (98.4°F).
○ The skeleton weighs about one fifth of the total body weight.
○ The body contains over 50 million million cells.
○ More men than women are colour-blind; most colour-blind people cannot tell red from green.

The Plant World

Just as animals are classified according to their common basic structures, so are plants. The main groups are called divisions, and each division is then broken down into a subdivision, a class, an order, a family, a genus and a species.

Classification of the Tea Rose

Division	Spermatophyta
Subdivision	Angiospermae
Class	Dicotyledonae
Order	Rosales
Family	Rosaceae
Genus	*Rosa*
Species	*Rosa adorata*

Examples of Divisions and their Characteristics

Division	Subdivision	Characteristics
Thallophyta		primitive plants with no clear distinction of roots, stems or leaves
	Algae	possess chlorophyll which produces the green colour in plants; make their own food; live in soil and water; includes seaweed (about 18,000 species)

Division	Subdivision	Characteristics
	Bacteria	minute single-celled organisms found in living and dead animals and plants; some beneficial to man, some harmful
	Fungi	cannot make food but obtain it from living or dead animals and plants; composed of thousands of fine threads; some beneficial to man, some harmful; 100,000 species known
	Lichens	plants growing on walls or bare rocks; a combination of a species of fungus living with a particular algae; grows very slowly
Bryophota		slight differentiation of plants into leaves and stems, but no true roots; needs moist environment; reproduces by spores
	Mosses	small green plants growing on trees, rocks and moist ground with many separate plants in each tuft; about 15,000 known species
	Liverworts	groups of yellowish-brown, red, green or purple plants growing on the ground, not unlike mosses in appearance; over 10,000 known species
Pteridophyta		ferns or related plants without seeds and reproduce by spores; leaves, stems and roots
	Ferns	distinguished by fronds; grow in moist places and found mainly on land but some in water; about 10,000 species

Division	Subdivision	Characteristics
	Horsetails	small leaves arranged in circles around a jointed stem; usually found in poor, sandy soils but occasionally in marshy conditions
	Clubmosses	evergreen plants with numerous leaves arranged in spirals; found everywhere but particularly in warm, wet environments; about 200 known species
Spermatophyta		seed bearing; clear divisions of leaves, stems and roots
	Gymnosperms	without flowers, but many with cones; includes evergreen trees
	Angiosperms	flowering plants with seeds within an ovary; includes flowering trees, flowers vegetables and grasses; about 250,000 known species

Trees and Plants

Many of the trees and plants we see growing are not native to this country. They were brought here by keen botanists two or three hundred years ago. At the same time, species from this country were taken to other countries, particularly by those settling in the Commonwealth.

Tree	Region of Origin
Alder, Common	Europe, North Africa, Western Asia
Beech	Europe–Western USSR
Cherry, Japanese	China, Japan
Chestnut, Horse	South Eastern Europe, Iran, USSR
Chestnut, Sweet (Spanish)	Southern Europe

Tree	Region of Origin
Elm, English	England
Elm, Smooth	Central and Southern Europe
Laburnum	Central and Southern Europe
Magnolia	Asia and North America
Maidenhair (Ginko)	Japan
Maple, Common	Europe, Asia Minor, Western Asia
Medlar	Iran, South-Eastern Europe
Monkey Puzzle	Chile
Mulberry, Common	Iran
Mulberry, Paper	China, Japan
Mulberry, Red	North America
Oak, Common	Europe, Asia, Urals (USSR)
Oak, Cork	Southern Europe, North Africa
Oak, Spanish	Southern USA
Olive	Southern Europe, North Africa
Poplar, Black	Europe, Western Asia
Rowan (Mountain Ash)	Europe–Caucasus (USSR)
Spruce, Black	Canada, North Eastern USA
Tulip Tree	Eastern North America
Walnut, Black	North America
Walnut, Common	Europe–China
Yew, Common	Europe–Himalayas

Some Facts About Trees

○ The Maidenhair tree (Ginko) is the world's oldest flowering plant, and first appeared about 180 million years ago.

○ The oldest recorded tree is a Bristlecone pine found on the Wheeler Ridge on the Sierra Nevada, California, USA, which is estimated to be 4,900 years old. The oldest recorded *living* tree is another Californian Bristlecone pine, now 4,600 years old.

○ The most massive tree in the world is the Giant Sequoia ('General Sherman') in the Sequoia National Park in California. Its estimated weight is 6,100 tonnes, its girth is 24.32 m, and it is 83 m high.

○ The oldest trees in England are yews. The yew in the churchyard at Fortingall in Tayside is thought to be 2,500 years old.

○ The largest natural forest in the world – covering 1,100 million hectares – is in northern USSR.

○ The largest man-made forest in the world – covering 151,096 hectares – is the Kaingaroa State Forest in New Zealand.

Origin of Some Flowers and Herbs

Flower	Region of Origin
Chrysanthemum	Japan, China
Cosmos	Mexico
Crocus	Southern Europe, Asia Minor
Dahlia	Mexico
Foxglove	Europe, Western Asia
Hyacinth	Asia Minor, Balkans, Greece
Lavender	Western Mediterranean
Lobelia	Africa, some species in Europe
Marigold	Mexico
Sunflower	Central America, Peru
Tulip	Mediterranean, Asia Minor
Wistaria	China
Zinnia	Mexico

Herbs and Spices	Place of Origin
Allspice	West Indies, Central America
Aniseed	Middle East, Greece, Asia Minor
Basil	India
Bay	Mediterranean
Borage	Mediterranean
Caraway	Middle East
Chervil	South-East Europe
Cinnamon	Sri Lanka
Cloves	East Indies
Coriander	Southern Europe, Asia
Ginger	South-East Asia, China
Mace	East Indies
Marjoram	Mediterranean
Nutmeg	East Indies
Pepper	India (West Coast)
Rosemary	Mediterranean
Saffron	Asia Minor
Tarragon	USSR
Thyme	Asia Minor, Mediterranean
Vanilla	Mexico

4 MAN'S DEVELOPMENT

Man

If you really think about prehistoric man, you will realise that survival was all-important. He needed food, water and shelter and, in some parts of the world, heat. He had to become cleverer than any other animal in order to survive.

There was so much to learn. He found that living in groups meant a greater chance of survival, but this also meant that he had to conform to some sort of social system. Because he had to communicate with others, he first developed language and then learned to write. The elements of nature were a mystery. Why were there floods or thunderstorms? He didn't know, and so he believed in supernatural forces, and religions were born.

Time was a mystery also, and so were seasons. He got up when the sun rose and went to bed when it set, but why did it vary throughout the year? He didn't know, but he began to measure it.

Men travelled, and as they travelled they both fought and traded. Empires rose and fell, but the traders went on trading. At first, trade meant barter, but this was an unsatisfactory way of dealing and so coinage based on gold and silver was introduced.

And so – step by step – man developed a social system, a means of communication, religion, a sense of time and seasons, an economic system, coinage, and a knowledge of the wider world.

Early Man

We all belong to the same species, *Homo sapiens*. The colour of our skin, the texture of our hair and our facial and physical characteristics are unimportant. It is what we have in common that matters – an upright posture, a large rounded skull, a well-developed intelligence and the ability to communicate verbally.

Modern man and modern apes are almost certainly descended

from the same common ancestor which, in turn, probably evolved from primitive mammals. This ape-like creature eventually came down from the trees and learned to walk upright. His brain developed, he learned to speak, and he used very simple tools and weapons; but all these developments took millions of years to evolve.

Type	Characteristics
Australopithecus	an ape-like creature known to have lived in southern and central Africa, some occupying limestone caves; probably under 1.5 m tall with huge jaws and teeth
Homo erectus	similar height but with a larger brain capacity and a smaller jaw than *Australopithecus*, prominent eyebrows, receding forehead
Homo neanderthalensis	a little taller that *Homo erectus* with a brain as large as ours, short legs, a low forehead and a small jaw; used tools, buried his dead, lived in Europe, Asia and Africa; gave way to *Homo sapiens*

Prehistoric Man

The table below shows how man gradually learned to live in larger communities and the skills he acquired, but it is only a rough guide since, in some parts of the world, he advanced more quickly than in others.

Period	Development	Years BC
Palaeolithic (lower)	(*Australopithecus* and *Homo erectus*) small nomadic groups of hunters and food gatherers; very simple stone tools and weapons	1,500,000
Palaeolithic (middle)	(*Homo neanderthalensis*) larger groups of hunters; flint tools, sometimes occupying caves	100,000
Palaeolithic (upper)	(*Homo sapiens*) larger hunting communities sometimes living in primitive huts and caves; bows and arrows, throwing sticks	40,000

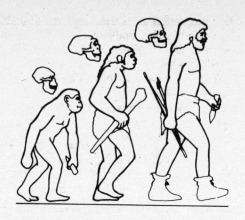

Period	Development	Years BC
Mesolithic	only partly nomadic communities; stone tools, harpoons and fishing nets, simple boats and sledges	10,000
Neolithic	farming communities, grain growing with domesticated animals; bone and wooden tools and weapons, pottery and weaving	7,500
Bronze Age	large villages and small towns but city-states in some areas; metal tools and weapons, wheeled carts; widespread trading, coinage	2,500
Iron Age	fortified towns in Europe; expansion of empires in the Middle and Near East; use of iron for weapons and tools, horses used for work and riding	2,000

Some Facts About Early Man

Date BC	
o 7,500	dogs domesticated
o 6,000	llamas domesticated in southern Peru, Bolivia and northern Chile
o 6,000	cattle domesticated in northern Greece
o 6,000	pigs domesticated in south-west Asia

o	5,700	maize cultivated in Tehuacan Valley in central Mexico
	5,000	sheep domesticated in Anau in Russian Turkestan; probably domesticated much earlier in the Near and Middle East
o	4,300	cotton grown in the Tehuacan Valley
o	4,000	plough in use in the Near East
o	3,400	both the wheel and the potter's wheel in use in the Near East
o	3,000	plank boats constructed in Egypt

Language

Language enables man to communicate thoughts and feelings by means of vocal sounds and by the use of written symbols of the sounds. Language is something that is common to a particular nation or tribe. Dialect is a variation of that language spoken by a small group of people in a particular region.

The Top Ten Languages

Language	Speakers (million)	Most Important Regions where Spoken
Mandarin Chinese	500	North and East Central China
English	320	UK, USA, Ireland, South Africa, Commonwealth
Hindi	170	North Central India
Russian	170	Widely spoken throughout Russia, but another hundred languages used
Spanish	140	Spain, Central and South America (not Brazil, and not the language of the majority in Bolivia, Ecuador, Guatemala and Peru)
Portuguese	120	Portugal, Brazil
Japanese	110	Japan
German	100	Austria, East Germany, West Germany, Switzerland
Bengali	90	Bangladesh, East India
Arabic	80	Middle East, North Africa

Writing

Long before man learned to write, he scratched pictures on cave walls and pieces of stone and bone. Most cave paintings show animals, and these are believed to be connected with hunting magic. By drawing its picture, the hunter believed that he had captured something of the spirit of the animal and weakened it, so that it would be easier to catch. Later, man attempted to pass on warnings and messages, and so pictures gave way to symbols.

Cuneiform Writing

The Sumerians originally drew pictures, but these were later represented by simpler curved lines. The Assyrians and Babylonians adopted this form of writing, which eventually gave way to wedge-shaped characters scratched onto soft, moist clay with a stylus made of bone or metal. Then the tablets were baked, so that they became practically indestructible.

Hieroglyphics

This form of script was developed by the Ancient Egyptians as early as 3,000 BC and it remained in use until 400 AD. At first, simple pictures expressed simple ideas, but the script soon became more sophisticated. Pictograms or ideograms showed the whole word in a picture, and phonograms represented the sound of words. The stem of a papyrus plant was used to make a kind of paper, and a hollow reed served as a pen.

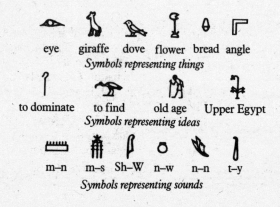

eye giraffe dove flower bread angle
Symbols representing things

to dominate   to find   old age   Upper Egypt
Symbols representing ideas

m–n   m–s   Sh–W   n–w   n–n   t–y
Symbols representing sounds

For centuries people puzzled over the meaning of hieroglyphics, but it wasn't until 1828 that Jean-François Champollion of France discovered the key when he was studying the inscriptions on the Rosetta Stone which had been found at Rosetta, in the Nile Delta.

Chinese Writing

Since Chinese writing was not phonetic, people had to learn many thousands of characters in order to learn to read and write. Now, a new simplified system has been introduced with a list of only about 2,000 characters. The Chinese made a further significant change in January 1966: the characters used to be read vertically from right to left, but books and newspapers appeared with the characters printed horizontally from left to right. A phonetic alphabet using twenty-five letters of the Roman alphabet and based on the Peking dialect (Mandarin) is now in use.

Alphabets

By about 1,500 BC, the first alphabet, a collection of signs representing the sounds of speech and arranged in a fixed order, was invented. Within 500 years there were four main alphabets, and each of these gave rise to many more.

HEBREW

מנסטעפצקרשתthחזוהדגבאעשטיסרכב

CYRILLIC

АБВГДЕЖЗИЙКЛМНОПР
СТУФХЦЧШЩЪЫЬЭЮЯ

ARABIC

ظظغغغغفتقققف قاككككاك لللللممممبن
على كى كى ىا ى مى س مىلا ()!؛٩٨٧٦٥٤٣٢١

GREEK

ΑΒΓΔΕΖΗΘΙΚΛΜΝΞΟΠΡΣΤΥΦΧΨΩ

Braille

Braille, invented by Louis Braille in 1834, is an alphabet which enables the blind to read. Each letter of the alphabet consists of one or more raised dots, and it has thirty-seven other signs to indicate figures, punctuation, and some for common words or parts of words.

Manual Alphabet

The deaf have several methods of communicating. One is the hand, or manual, alphabet. This, when used in conjunction with sign language, enables them to 'speak' with great rapidity.

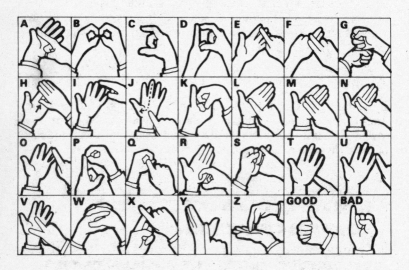

Other Forms of Communication

Semaphore

Before the telegraph was invented, people had a problem when they wanted to pass on a message quickly but were too far away to shout to each other! Various methods of communication were tried and the most successful was the use of the semaphore code invented in 1822.

Semaphore stations were set up. These were posts with mechanical arms – the position of the arms denoting the letters of the

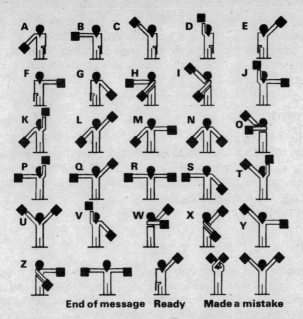

End of message Ready Made a mistake

alphabet. Later, it was realized that messages could be transmitted in the same way but by using hand-held flags instead of the mechanical arms. For the first seven letters and the numbers one to seven, only one flag is used. Two flags are used for all other letters and numbers.

Morse Code

Wireless telegraphy is a way of transmitting messages by the opening and closing of an electrical circuit with a key. Samuel Morse

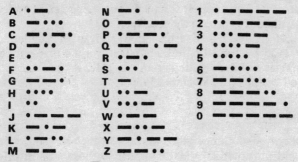

invented an alphabet in which the letters are combinations of dots and dashes, the dash being a longer signal than the dot. As well as letters and numbers, the code also uses combinations of letters as punctuation marks. The Morse code is also used with flags and with flashing lights.

Telephones

The telephone was invented by Alexander Graham Bell in 1876. It is a system which conveys speech over distances by the use of a receiver and a transmitter connected by an electrical conductor. Speech is converted into variable electrical impulses which flow through the circuit and are translated back into sounds by the receiver. In 1879 the first telephone exchange was opened in London.

Radio

The radio was originally known as the wireless since it communicated electrical signals without the use of wires. Sounds and signals are converted into electromagnetic waves which are transmitted into a receiver and then changed back into sounds.

Guglielmo Marconi developed the work started by James Clerk Maxwell and Heinrich Hertz on electromagnetic waves, and in 1896 he succeeded in establishing a connection between Penarth and Weston-super-Mare. The invention of the radio valve by Fleming in 1904 paved the way for broadcasting which began in Britain in 1920.

Television

Television is the transmission of visible moving images by electrical means. Light waves are converted into electrical impulses by a television camera and appear as a picture on the screen of a television set via a cathode ray tube in the receiver.

The first practical demonstration was given in London on 27 January 1926 by John Logie Baird. The world's first public television service was transmitted from the BBC station at Alexandra Palace in London on 2 November 1936.

Typewriters

Typewriters are machines with a keyboard which reproduces letters, figures and punctuation symbols similar to those used in printing.

When the key is struck, raised letters on bars are pressed against a ribbon thus making an impression on paper inserted into the machine.

The first practicable typewriter was built in 1867. Tabulators appeared in 1898, portable machines round about 1912, and electric typewriters in 1940.

The latest development is that of the word processor – computers programmed to deal with text. The computer allows the operator to correct mistakes, to reshape sentences, paragraphs or pages, and print the text, as well as storing it on a tape or a disc.

Computers

Computers are electronic machines that accept information, apply logical processes to it, and supply an answer. The first fully electronic computer was ENIAC, built in 1946, which was so huge that it filled a large room. It used so many thermionic valves that it soon overheated and burned out. Once transistors were invented, computers became much smaller and far more reliable.

There are two main kinds of computers: digital computers, in which numbers are expressed directly as digits, usually binary; and analog computers, in which numbers are presented by magnitudes of physical quantities, such as voltages.

Abbreviations

Latin and French Phrases in Common Use

Phrase	Abbreviation	Meaning
ad infinitum		Latin: forever, limitless
ad libitum	ad lib	Latin: to the extent desired, to improvise
ad majorem dei gloriam	A.M.D.G.	Latin: to the greater glory of God
ad nauseam		Latin: to the point of disgust
à la carte		French: from the menu; individually priced dishes
anno domini	A.D.	Latin: in the year of our Lord
anno mundi	A.M.	Latin: in the year of the world

Phrase	Abbreviation	Meaning
ante meridiem	a.m.	Latin: before noon
circa	c.	Latin: about
de facto		Latin: in fact; regardless of legal or moral consideration
Deo gratias		Latin: thanks to God
déjà vu		French: the impression of having had an experience previously
de jure		Latin: by right, in accordance with law
Deo volente	D.V.	Latin: God willing
dernier cri		French: the latest fashion; the last word
de rigeur		French: required by etiquette
de trop		French: unwanted, superfluous
et alia	et al	Latin: and others
et cetera	etc.	Latin: and the like, and other things
et sequentia	et seq	Latin: and the following
exempli gratia	e.g.	Latin: for the sake of example
ex-libris	ex lib	Latin: from the books of
fecit	fec.	Latin: he/she did it, made it
fidei defensor	F.D.	Latin: defender of the faith
floruit	fl.	Latin: he/she flourished
faux pas		French: a social mistake, a tactless remark or act
ibidem	ibid	Latin: in the same place
idem quod	i.q.	Latin: the same as
id est	i.e.	Latin: that is
in loco	in loc.	Latin: in its place
nota bene	n.b.	Latin: note well
non sequitur	non seq.	Latin: it does not follow
numero	no.	Latin: number
opere citato	op. cit.	Latin: in the work cited
per annum	p.a.	Latin: by the year, yearly
per capita		Latin: for each person

Phrase	Abbreviation	Meaning
per centum	per cent	Latin: in, to, or for each hundred, by the hundred
per diem		Latin: by the day, daily
per procurationem	per pro.	Latin: by proxy
per se		Latin: by or in itself, inherently
post meridiem	p.m.	Latin: afternoon
pourboire		French: a tip
pour prendre congé	P.P.C.	French: to take leave
post scriptum	P.S.	Latin: postscript
pro tempore	pro tem.	Latin: for the time being
proximo	prox.	Latin: next month
quod erat demonstrandum	Q.E.D.	Latin: which was to be proved
quod erat faciendum	q.e.f.	Latin: which was to be done
quod vide	q.v.	Latin: which see
quo jure		Latin: by what right
répondez, s'il vous plaît	R.S.V.P.	French: please reply
sic		Latin: so written
stet		Latin: let it stand
ultimo	ult.	Latin: in the preceding month
versus	v.	Latin: against
verbum sapienti satis est	verb. sap.	Latin: a word to the wise is enough
videlicet	viz.	Latin: namely

Abbreviations Used for Honours

Abbreviation	Honour
CB	Companion of the Most Honourable Order of the Bath
CBE	Commander of the British Empire
CH	Companion of Honour
DCB	Dame Commander of the Most Honourable Order of the Bath
DCMG	Dame Commander of the Order of St Michael and St George
DCVO	Dame Commander of the Royal Victorian Order

Abbreviation	Honour
GCB	Dame/Knight of the Grand Cross of the Most Honourable Order of the Bath
GCMG	Dame/Knight Grand Cross of the Order of St Michael and St George
GCVO	Dame/Knight Grand Cross of the Royal Victorian Order
ISO	Imperial Service Order
KBE	Knight Commander of the British Empire
KCB	Knight Commander of the Most Honourable Order of the Bath
KCG	Knight Companion of the Garter
KCVO	Knight Commander of the Royal Victorian Order
KG	Knight of the Garter
KT	Knight of the Most Ancient and Most Noble Order of The Thistle
MBE	Member of the British Empire
MVO	Member of the Royal Victorian Order
OBE	Officer of the British Empire
OM	Order of Merit

Abbreviations: Some Institutions and Associations

When the institution or society is preceded by the letters M or F, it means that someone is a member or fellow. A indicates an associate.

Abbreviaton	Society or Institution
AA	Alcoholics' Anonymous
AA	Architectural Association
AA	Automobile Association
AAAS	American Association for the Advancement of Science
BMA	British Medical Association
BTA	British Tourist Association
CAB	Citizen's Advice Bureaux
CCPR	Central Council for Physical Recreation
CND	Campaign for Nuclear Disarmament
COSIRA	Council for Small Industries in Rural Areas
FPA	Family Planning Association

Abbreviaton	Society or Institution
ICE	Institution of Civil Engineers
NNCL	National Council for Civil Liberties
NSPCA	National Society for the Prevention of Cruelty to Animals
NSPCC	National Society for the Prevention of Cruelty to Children
NT	National Trust
PA	Press Association
PDSA	People's Dispensary for Sick Animals
PTA	Parent Teacher Association
RA	Royal Academy
RAC	Royal Automobile Club
RCN	Royal College of Nursing
RCP	Royal College of Physicians
RCPS	Royal College of Physicians and Surgeons
RCVS	Royal College of Vetinary Surgeons
RGS	Royal Geographical Society
RHA	Royal Historical Society
RHS	Royal Horticultural Society
RIBA	Royal Institute of British Architects
RICS	Royal Institution of Chartered Surveyors
RNLI	Royal National Lifeboat Institution
RSC	Royal Society of Chemists
RSPCA	Royal Society for the Prevention of Cruelty to Animals
RSPB	Royal Society for the Protection of Birds
RSPCC	Royal Society for the Prevention of Cruelty to Children
YHA	Youth Hostels Association
YMCA	Young Men's Christian Association
YWCA	Young Women's Christian Association

Abbreviations: Some Members of the Trades Union Congress (TUC)

Abbreviation	Trade Union	Number of Members (to nearest thousand)
ACTAT	Association of Cinematograph, Television and Allied Technicians	25,000
ASLEF	Associated Society of Locomotive Engineers and Firemen	23,000
AUEW	Amalgamated Union of Engineering Workers	1,001,000
APEX	Association of Professional, Executive, Clerical and Computer Staff	95,000
ASTMS	Association of Scientific, Technical and Managerial Staff	400,000
AUT	Association of University Teachers	32,000
BALPA	British Air Line Pilots Association	4,000
BIFU	Banking, Insurance and Finance Union	155,000
COHSE	Confederation of Health Service Employees	214,000
CPSA	Civil and Public Services Association	150,000
EETPU	Electrical, Electronic, Telecommunication and Plumbing Union	394,000
GMW	General Municipal Boilermakers and Allied Trades Union	847,000
IPCS	Institution of Professional Civil Servants	90,000
IRSF	Inland Revenue Staff Federation	55,000
ISTC	Iron and Steel Trades Confederation	79,000
NALGO	National and Local Government Officers' Association	766,000
NAS/UWT	National Association of Schoolmasters/Union of Women Teachers	126,000
NCU	National Communications Union	166,000

Abbreviation	Trade Union	Number of Members (to nearest thousand)
NGA	National Graphical Association	126,000
NUJ	National Union of Journalists	33,000
NUM	National Union of Mineworkers	200,000
NUPE	National Union of Public Employees	673,000
NUR	National Union of Railwaymen	136,000
NUS	National Union of Seamen	25,000
NUT	National Union of Teachers	214,000
SCPS	Society of Civil and Public Servants	86,000
SOGAT	Society of Graphical and Allied Trades	210,000
TWU	Transport and General Workers' Union	1,491,000

Religion

The Ancient World

Primitive man was superstitious because there was so much that he didn't understand. He didn't know why the sun rose or set, what caused thunder, what an eclipse was or why the seasons changed, and so he chose to worship something, like the sun or a river, and he carried out ceremonies to please it.

Gradually, this worship became more formal. Gods and goddesses were given names, and they ruled specific areas and performed particular tasks.

Greek and Roman Gods and Goddesses

Greek	Roman	Function
Zeus	Jupiter	supreme god
Hera	Juno	wife of supreme god, goddess of women
Poseidon	Neptune	god of the sea
Aphrodite	Venus	goddess of love
Artemis	Diana	goddess of the moon
Eros	Cupid	god of love

Greek	Roman	Function
Mercury	Hermes	messenger of the gods
Asclepius	Aesculapius	god of medicine and healing
Hephaestus	Vulcan	god of fire and metal-working
Nestia	Vesta	goddess of the hearth and fire
Ares	Mars	god of war
Irene	Pax	goddess of peace
Dionysus	Bacchus	god of wine and revelry
Hypnos	Somnus	god of sleep
Athena	Minerva	goddess of wisdom
Pan	Faunus	god of the fields, forests, wild animals, flocks and shepherds

Gods of Some Other Civilizations

Hindu	Function
Brahma	supreme spirit of the universe
Vishnu	the preserver
Shiva	god of destruction
Varuna	god of the heavens
Agni	god of fire and the hearth
Surya	sun god

Egypt	Function
Osiris	god of the lower world, judge of the dead
Isis	wife of Osiris, goddess of fertility
Re	sun god
Thoth	god of learning and magic, the measurer of time
Hathor	goddess of love and joy
Tauret	goddess of childbirth
Maat	goddess of truth and divine order

Norse	Function
Odin	supreme god
Thor	god of thunder
Tyr (Tui)	god of war
Frigg	goddess of heaven, marriage and the home
Freya	goddess of love and beauty

Monotheism

Monotheism is the belief in only one god. For thousands of years the people of the ancient civilizations worshipped many gods, often adopting each others' if they seemed a good idea. Then, in Persia during the seventh century BC, Zarathustra taught that above all good and bad spirits there was a supreme creator of the universe, Ahura Mazda, and he urged men to stop the worship of many gods. The Persian king, Darius, encouraged him, and his successor, Xerxes, suppressed the old religion, but after about sixty years, the people returned to polytheism.

The next people to believe in one god were the Jews, and they were followed by the Christians. Another type of montheism arose in Arabia in the seventh century AD, when Mohammed taught that Allah was the sole creator of the universe.

Some Religions of the World

Religion	Number (millions)	Main Areas Practised	Belief
Buddhism	200	South-East Asia	self-denial, right-thinking and right-living will enable the soul to reach Nirvana, a divine state free from bodily pain, sorrow and desire

Religion	Number (millions)	Main Areas Practised	Belief
Christianity	1,000	Europe, North and South America, Australasia, South Africa, parts of Central and East Africa, Greece, Philippines	belief in God, that Jesus Christ was his son and that he rose from the dead and returned to God; belief in the Holy Spirit
Confucianism	300	China	teachings emphasize ancestor worship, devotion to parents and the family, and the maintenance of justice and peace.
Hinduism	500	India	tolerance and the belief that people are reincarnated; those living bad lives will be re-born in a lower state, while the good will be re-born in a higher state and may eventually be absorbed into the life of God.

Religion	Number (millions)	Main Areas Practised	Belief
Judaism	18	Israel, also many other parts of the world	belief in Jehovah who gave the Jews the Torah (the Law) as a way of life, that man does not need a mediator between himself and God, that all have equal rights and duties, and that knowledge is of the utmost importance
Islam	600	North Africa, Arabia and the Gulf, Central and East Africa, Pakistan, India, Turkey, Indonesia and elsewhere	belief that Allah is the creator, that he is supreme, that nothing happens except by his will and that he is merciful; belief in prayer, fasting, almsgiving and pilgrimage; that good and bad deeds are recorded and will be balanced against each other on the day of judgement

World Council of Churches

This organization was formed to promote unity between all Christian churches. The 303 churches represent Christians in over 100 countries. The Assembly meets every seven years and the Central Committee annually.

Celebrations

Calendar of Patron Saints

Date	Saint	Protects
14 January	St Sava	Serbian people
19 January	St Yves	journalists and writers
24 January	St Francis de Sales	lawyers
28 January	St Peter Molasco	midwives
3 February	St Blaise	those with sore throats
5 February	St Agatha	bell-founders
9 February	St Apollonia	those with toothache
14 February	St Valentine	lovers
1 March	St David	Wales
8 March	St John of God	nurses and the sick
17 March	St Patrick	Ireland
23 April	St George	England
25 April	St Mark	Venice
15 May	St Hallvard	Oslo
28 May	St Bernard of Montjoux	Alpinists and other mountaineers
29 May	St Bona of Pisa	couriers, guides and air hostesses
30 May	St Hubert	hunters and trappers
2 June	St Erasmus of Elmo	sailors
13 June	St Anthony of Padua	careless people
29 June	St Peter	fishermen
29 June	St Martha	housewives and those serving the needy
11 July	St Benedict	Europe
14 July	St Camillus	nurses and the sick
25 July	St Christopher	travellers and motorists
24 August	St Bartholomew	beekeepers
1 September	St Fiacre	cab drivers
27 September	St Cosmas and St Damian	physicians
28 September	St Wenceslas	Czechoslovakia
29 September	St Michael the Archangel	soldiers
4 October	St Francis of Assissi	ecologists
9 October	St Denis	France

Date	Saint	Protects
16 October	St Luke	physicians and surgeons
25 October	St Crispin and St Crispinian	shoemakers
3 November	St Hubert	animals
6 November	St Leonard	prisoners
11 November	St John the Almsgiver	Order of St John of Jerusalem (later the Knights of Malta)
15 November	St Albert the Great	students of natural sciences
17 November	St Elizabeth of Hungary	queens
22 November	St Cecilia	music
30 November	St Andrew	Scotland
1 December	St Eligius	metal workers
3 December	St Francis Xavier	Roman Catholic missionaries abroad
6 December	St Nicholas	children
13 December	St Lucy	those with eye diseases

Wedding Anniversaries

In many countries special gifts are given to mark the occasion of a wedding anniversary. Some of the best known are included below:

No. Years Married	Gift	No. Years Married	Gift
1	cotton	15	crystal
2	paper	20	china
3	leather	25	silver
4	silk	30	pearl
5	wool	35	coral
6	sweets	40	ruby
7	wood	45	sapphire
8	bronze	50	gold
9	pottery	55	emerald
10	tin	60	diamond

Precious and Semi-precious Stones

Some people associate precious and semi-precious stones with months of the year and consider them birthstones; others prefer to consider those associated with astrological signs as birthstones.

Stone	Characteristics
agate	hard semi-precious stone with striped or clouded colouring; a kind of chalcedony which is a type of quartz
aquamarine	a transparent pale, bluish-green variety of beryl
amethyst	a kind of quartz, usually violet or purple in colour
bloodstone	a semi-precious dark green form of quartz spotted with red jasper
diamond	one of the hardest substances known, a crystalline form of carbon of great brilliance; only twenty per cent of those found are suitable as gem stones
emerald	a transparent or transluscent green variety of beryl; the best come from Colombia
garnet	a stone of varying composition but usually double silicates of calcium or aluminium with other metals; the best are a deep transparent red but can be green or other colours
opal	glassy silicas of various colours; the commonest are an opaque milky-white, yellow, red-blue or green; fire opals have flamelike colours, the best from Mexico; black opals have a dark-green background and come from New South Wales in Australia
pearl	calcareous substance secreted by molluscs , e.g. oysters, deposited round irritant bodies; hard, smooth and lustrous in appearance
ruby	a gem stone of red transparent corundum, the best found in Burma
sapphire	clear deep-blue form of carborundum, the best from Ceylon and Burma; green or colourless sapphires are of less value
sardonyx	a kind of chalcedony with alternate layers of white and deep orange.
topaz	an aluminium silicate varying in colour from yellow to white, pale-blue, pale-green and pink, the best from Brazil, Peru and Ceylon

Stone	Characteristics
turquoise	composed of hydrous phosphate of aluminium with small amounts of copper, bluish-green or sky-blue, the best from Turkestan, Persia and Mexico

Birthstones

Month	Stone	Astrological Sign	Stone
January	garnet	Aquarius	amethyst
February	amethyst	Pisces	bloodstone
March	bloodstone	Aries	diamond
April	diamond	Taurus	emerald
May	emerald	Gemini	agate
June	pearl	Cancer	ruby
July	ruby	Leo	sardonyx
August	sardonyx	Virgo	sapphire
September	sapphire	Libra	opal
October	opal	Scorpio	topaz
November	topaz	Sagittarius	turquoise
December	turquoise	Capricorn	garnet

Signs of the Zodiac

The zodiac is an imaginary belt in the heavens which follows the path of the Sun and is divided into twelve equal areas containing twelve constellations. These are represented by symbols. No one knows when they were adopted, but some have been traced back 3,000 years.

Aries the Ram
21 March–20 April

Gemini the Twins
22 May–21 June

Taurus the Bull
21 April–21 May

Cancer the Crab
22 June–22 July

Leo the Lion
23 July–23 August

Sagittarius the Archer
23 November–23 December

Virgo the Virgin
24 August–23 September

Capricorn the Goat
22 December–20 January

Libra the Scales
24 September–23 October

Aquarius the Water Carrier
21 January–19 February

Scorpio the Scorpion
24 October–22 November

Pisces the Fish
20 February–20 March

The Seven Wonders of the World

These were listed by Antipater of Sidon in the second century BC.
Only the Pyramids still stand.

Name	Description
Pyramids of Giza	monumental tombs in the shape of pentahedrons built for the Egyptian pharaohs Cheops (Khufu), Chefren (Khefren) and Mykerinus; the Great Pyramid of Cheops, 230 m long on each side and 147 m high, was completed about 2,580 BC

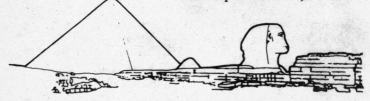

Temple of Artemis (Diana) at Ephesus	constructed in Ephesus in Turkey in 350 BC and destroyed by the Goths in 262 AD
Tomb of King Mausolus of Caria	a magnificent mausoleum built in 325 BC in Halicarnassus (now Bodrum) in Turkey
Hanging Gardens of Babylon	originally known as the Hanging Gardens of Semiramis built in Babylon in Iraq about 600 BC
Statue of Zeus at Olympia	the gold, marble and ivory 12 m tall statute of the Greek god Zeus was the work of Phidias; it was executed in the fifth century BC and was destroyed in a fire
Colossus of Rhodes	the 35 m tall statue of the god Helios (Apollo) by Chares of Lindus executed between 292 and 280 BC was destroyed in an earthquake in 224 BC
Pharos of Alexandria	the world's first lighthouse, 122 m tall, was built by Sostratus of Cnidus in 270 BC and destroyed in an earthquake in 1375 AD

Time

The Egyptians were almost certainly the first people to make artificial divisions of time by inventing the hour. To mark the passing of time they used an upright stick and noted the length and position of its shadow, thus inventing a kind of sundial. At night they used the clepsydra, a water clock.

Much later, in northern Europe, there were sundials but these are useless if there is no sun, and so sand-timers were used. There was a real step forward in 1275 when a clock producing a single note on a bell, was invented. The first known public clock was erected in Milan in 1335.

The Calendar

A calendar is a way of determining the beginning, divisions and length of a year.

A calendar day is 24 hours long and runs from one midnight to the next.

A calendar month is any one of the 12 divisions of a year.

A calendar year is the period of time from 1 January to 31 December.

The Julian Calendar was introduced by Julius Caesar in 46 BC. This gave an ordinary year of 365 days and 366 days on every fourth year. However, this was not accurate enough, and was incorrect by one day in every 128 years.

The Gregorian Calendar, introduced by Pope Gregory XIII in 1582, corrected the mistake in the Julian Calendar. In this calendar, ordinary years have 365 days and every fourth year has 366 excluding century years unless they are divisible by 400.

Leap years are those which have 366 days. The extra day is added on to the end of February so that it has 29 days instead of 28.

Months of the Year

It is important to remember that in the Julian calendar months were reckoned from March.

Month	Length	Origin of Name
January	31	from the Latin, *Ianuarius*; named after Janus, the two-faced Roman god of beginnings
February	28 (29)	from the Latin, *Februarius*; the name stems from the root of *Februare* meaning 'to purify'; this was the Roman month of purification in readiness for the New Year (15 February was the Day of Purification)
March	31	from the Latin *Martius*; named after Mars, the Roman god of war
April	30	from the Latin, *Aprilis*; the month sacred to Venus, the Roman goddess of love; Aphrodite was the equivalent Greek goddess and so the name could derive from *aperire*, meaning 'to open' as buds and flowers do at this time of the year

Month	Length	Origin of Name
May	31	from the Latin, *Maius*, but origin uncertain; perhaps from *Maiores* meaning elders, perhaps from *Maia*, the goddess who represented increase
June	30	from the Latin, *Iunius*; origin unclear but it could be connected with the Roman goddess Juno or it might mean the time honouring the young and the favoured
July	31	from the Latin *Iulius*: named in honour of Julius Caesar in 44 BC following his assassination; originally it had been known as Quintilis, the fifth month
August	31	from the Latin *Augustus*: named in honour of the emperor Augustus in 8 BC; originally it had been known as Sextilis, the sixth month
September	30	from the Latin *Septem*: derived from *septem* meaning 'seven', and *imber*, a shower of rain reflecting the season of the year
October	31	from the Latin *Octo*: named after the eighth month of the year in the Roman calendar, since *octo* means eight.
November	30	from the Latin *Novem*: named after the ninth month of the year in the Roman calendar, since *novem* means nine
December	31	from the Latin *Decem*: named after the tenth month in the Roman calendar, since *decem* means ten

Days of the Week

A day lasts twenty-four hours – the time it takes the earth to revolve once on its axis.

Day	Origin of Name
Sunday	Anglo-Saxon *Sunnen daeg*: the first day of the week, meaning 'the day of the sun'
Monday	Anglo-Saxon *Monan daeg*: the second day of the week, meaning 'the day of the moon'

Day	Origin of Name
Tuesday	Anglo-Saxon *Tiwes daeg*: the third day of the week, named after Tiw, the god of war and son of Odin
Wednesday	Anglo-Saxon *Wodnes daeg*: the fourth day of the week, named after Woden (Odin). Odin was the supreme god in Norse mythology as well as being the god of art, culture and the dead
Thursday	Anglo-Saxon *Thunres daeg*: the fifth day of the week, named after Thor, the god of thunder and strength; Thursday in French is 'jeudi', Jove's day, and both Jove and Thor were gods of thunder
Friday	Anglo-Saxon *Frige daeg*: the sixth day of the week, named after Frigg or Freya, the goddess of love; the French word is 'vendredi' or the day of Venus, and both Freya and Venus were goddesses of love
Saturday	Anglo-Saxon *Saeter daeg*: the seventh day of the week, named after the Latin *Saturni dies*, 'Saturn's day'

Seasons of the Year

Each season of the year is associated with differences in the development of plants and changes in temperature, weather, and the hours of daylight. Astronomically, they are defined as beginning about 21 March, June, September and December.

Spring

Spring begins at the vernal equinox. This is the day when the sun crosses the equator making day and night of equal length. Roughly speaking, this covers the end of March until late June in the northern hemisphere.

Summer

Summer starts at the summer solstice. This is the time when the sun is at its greatest distance from the equator and when there is no variation between sunrise and sunset for several days. Summer covers the months from late June to mid-September in the northern hemisphere and from late December to late March in the southern hemisphere. Oddly enough, 21 June, the first day of summer in the northern hemisphere, is also known as Midsummer Day.

Autumn

Autumn begins at the autumnal equinox when the sun crosses from north to south of the equator, and night and day are almost of equal length. Strictly speaking, in the northern hemisphere it extends from 21 September to 22 December, and from 21 March to 21 June in the southern hemisphere, but in the USA it extends from September to November.

Winter

Winter is the coldest season of the year in the northern hemisphere and extends from the winter solstice to the spring equinox: 21 December to about 20 March. In the southern hemisphere it extends from about 22 June to 21 September.

World Time Chart

International Date Line

This is an internationally agreed time-change line drawn approximately along the 180° meridian, which zig-zags to avoid land in the Pacific Ocean. A crossing of the date line means repeating one day when travelling in an eastwards direction, and losing one day when travelling westwards. This compensates for a change of one hour for each 15° of longitude.

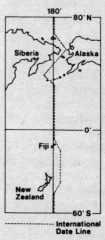

Area	Standard Time (difference in hours from GMT)
Afghanistan	+4.5
Albania	+1
Aleutian Islands	−11
Andaman Islands	+6.5
Angola	+1
Antigua	−4
Argentina	−4
Australia	
Victoria, Queensland, New South Wales, Tasmania	+10
Northern Territory, South Australia	+9.5

Austria	+1	Egypt	+2
Azores	−2	Ethiopia	+3
Bahamas	−5	Falkland Islands	−4
Bahrain	+3	Fiji	+12
Bangladesh	+6	Finland	+2
Barbados	−4		
Bermuda	−4	Germany	+1
Bolivia	−4	Greece	+2
Botswana	+2	Grenada	−4
Brazil		Guinea	−1
East	−3	Guyana	−3.75
West	−4		
Acre	−5	Haiti	−5
Brunei	+8	Honduras	−6
Bulgaria	+2	Hong Kong	+8
Burma	+6.5	Hungary	+1
Canada		India	+5.5
Atlantic Zone	−4	Indonesia	
Eastern Zone	−5	Western Zone	+7
Central Zone	−6	Central Zone	+8
Mountain Zone	−7	Eastern Zone	+9
Pacific Zone	−8	Iran	+3.5
Yukon Territory	−9	Iraq	+3
Cape Verde Islands	−2	Ireland	−1
Central African Republic	+1	Israel	+2
Chile	−4	Italy	+1
China			
Chungking, Lanchow	+7	Jamaica	−5
Peking, Shanghai	+8	Japan	+9
Christmas Island	+7	Jordan	+2
Cook Islands	−10.5		
Costa Rica	−6	Kalaadlit	
Cuba	−5	Scoresby Sound	−2
Cyprus	+2	West coast (not Thule)	−3
Czechoslovakia	+1	Thule	−4
		Kenya	+3
Denmark	+1	Korea	
Dominican Republic	−5	North Korea	+9
		Republic of Korea	+9
Ecuador	−5	Kuwait	+3

108

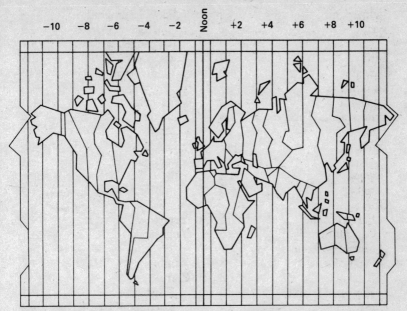

International time zones: hours behind and ahead of GMT

Lebanon	+2	Pakistan	+5
Leeward Islands	−4	Panama	−5
Libya	+1	Papua New Guinea	+10
		Paraguay	−4
Madeira	−1	Peru	−5
Malawi	+2	Philippine Islands	+8
Malaysia		Poland	+1
West Malaysia	+7.5	Puerto Rico	−4
East Malaysia	+8		
Maldive Islands	+5	Salvador	−6
Malta	+1	Santa Cruz Islands	+11
Mauritius	+4	Saudi Arabia	+3
Mexico	−7	Senegal	−1
Mozambique	+2	Seychelles	+4
		Singapore	+7.75
Nepal	+5.5	Solomon Islands	+11
New Guinea	+10	South Africa	+2
New Zealand	+12	Sri Lanka	+5.5
Nicaragua	−5.75	Sudan	+2
Norway	+1	Sweden	+1

Switzerland	+1	Kiev, Leningrad,	
Syria	+2	Moscow, Odessa	+3
		Archangel	+4
Tahiti	−10	Omsk	+6
Taiwan	+8	Vlodivostok	+10
Tanzania	+3		
Thailand	+7	Venezuela	−4.5
Trinidad and Tobago	−4	Vietnam	
Tunisia	+1	North	+7
Turkey	+2	South	+8
		Virgin Islands	−4
Uganda	+3		
Uruguay	−3.5	Windward Islands	−4
USA			
Eastern Zone	−5	Yemen	+3
Central Zone	−6	Yugoslavia	+1
Mountain Zone	−7		
Pacific Zone	−8	Zambia	+2
Alaska	−8	Zaire	
Hawaiian Islands	−10	Kinshasha	+1
USSR		Katanga, Kasai, Kivu	+2
Latvia	+2	Zimbabwe	+2

Exploration

By 18,000 BC man inhabited much of the world. He was already living in Africa, Alaska and Asia, including Japan, Australia and Europe, moving from place to place as the climate changed and the seas advanced or receded making it possible for him to travel.

When the ice sheets in the northern hemisphere retreated, the land bridge to North America was exposed, and Mongaloid hunters strayed into Canada in about 10,000 BC, wandered across America and down into Central America. By 8,500 BC they had reached South America.

Expeditions

Year	Explorer	Expedition
138 BC	Chang Chi'en (China)	makes his way to central Asia
AD 629	Hsuan Chuang (China)	walks to India; spends 631–33 in Kashmir
1100	Lief Eriksson (Vik)	son of Erik the Red, colonizes Greenland, discovers Vinland (probably Nova Scotia)
1275	Marco Polo (It)	reaches China, lives there for seventeen years, visits Persia etc.
1427	Johannes de Plana (It)	Franciscan friar travels to Mongolia
1469	Fernão Gomes (Port)	explores west coast of Africa
1482	Diogo Cão (Port)	explores west coast of Africa, reaches mouth of R. Zaire
1488	José Bartolomue (Port)	discovers Cape of Good Hope
1492	Christopher Columbus (It)	reaches America, discovers Watling Island, Cuba and Haiti
1493–6	Christopher Columbus	discovers Antigua, Guadeloupe, Jamaica, Montserrat and Puerto Rico
1497	John Cabot (It)	discovers Cape Breton Island
1497–9	Vasco de Gama (Port)	reaches India via the Cape of Good Hope and Natal

Year	Explorer	Expedition
1498	Christopher Columbus	discovers Trinidad, sights S. American mainland
1498	John Cabot	reaches Greenland
1499	Amerigo Vespucci (It)	sails along the north coast of Brazil, probably reaching Rio de la Plata
1502	Vasco de Gama	founds colony in Madagascar
1502–4	Christopher Columbus	explores the coast of Nicaragua and Honduras
1513	Juan Ponce de Léon (Sp)	reaches Florida, thinks it is an island
1518	Juan de Grijvalva (Sp)	sails along Mexican coast
1519	Alvarez Pineda (Sp)	explores Caribbean coast
1519	Ferdinand Magellan (Port)	attempts to reach the East Indies via the west; sails through the Magellan Straits; reaches and names the Pacific; reaches Guam and the Philippines where he is killed
1519–22	Juan de Elcanao (Sp)	with seventeen others from Magellan's expedition reaches Spain having circumnavigated the world
1524	Giovanni de Verrazzana (It)	explores North American coast and proves that North America is a continuous landmass

Year	Explorer	Expedition
1524	Francisco Hernandez de Cordoba (Sp)	explores Lake Nicaragua
1525–29	Sebastian Cabot (It)	explores Brazilian coast and Paraguay
1526–7	Francisco Pizarro (Sp)	explores north west coast of South America, five years later begins conquest of the Inca Empire
1534	Jacques Cartier (Fr)	enters the Gulf of St Lawrence and explores Canada as far as Montreal
1539	Hernando de Soto (Sp)	lands in Florida, makes his way to Oklahoma, discovers River Mississippi
1541–2	Gonzolo Pizarro (Sp)	explores the region east of Quito in Peru
1544	Sir Martin Frobisher (UK)	reaches Guinea
1576	Sir Martin Frobisher	seeking North West Passage, reaches Labrador and Frobisher Bay in Baffin Land
1577–80	Sir Francis Drake (UK)	first Englishman to circumnavigate the globe
1594–5	John Davis (UK)	discovers the Falkland Islands
1603	Samuel de Champlain (Fr)	first of several expeditions to Canada, founds Quebec in 1608
1608	Henry Hudson (UK)	attempts to reach China via the North West passage

Year	Explorer	Expedition
1609	Henry Hudson	reaches New York Bay and sails up the River Hudson
1612–3	Sir Thomas Button	reaches the western shore of Hudson Bay and discovers River Nelson
1615–6	Robert Bylot, William Baffin (UK)	discover Baffin Bay and Baffin Island
1615–6	Jakob le Maire (Neth)	sails through Le Maire Strait, rounds Cape Horn and discovers some of the Tonga group and Hoorn Islands
1617	William Baffin	surveys the Red Sea and the Persian Gulf
1642–3	Abel Tasman (Neth)	circumnavigates Australia, discovers New Zealand, Tonga and Fiji
1682	La Salle (Fr)	having surveyed River Illinois and River Mississippi, claims Louisiana for France
1722	Jacob Raggeveen (Neth)	discovers Easter Island
1728	Vitus Bering (Dan)	makes a reconnaisance of Alaska, sails through the Bering Strait to the Arctic
1768	James Cook (UK)	reaches Tahiti, charts New Zealand, makes a detailed survey of the east coast of Australia, surveys the Great Barrier Reef

Year	Explorer	Expedition
1772–5	James Cook	locates Easter Island, plots the Marquesas and Tonga Islands, discovers New Caledonia and Norfolk Island, returns to New Zealand
1776–9	James Cook	discovers some of the Cook Islands, rediscovers the Hawaiian Islands, reaches the American Pacific coast and surveys it as far as the Bering Strait, surveys the Siberian coast, returns to Hawaii where he is killed
1789	Sir Alexander Mackenzie (UK)	explores Canada, discovers the River Mackenzie
1795–7	Mungo Park (UK)	explores the River Niger
1800–4	Friedrich Humboldt (Germ)	explores the region of the River Orinoco
1801–3	Matthew Flinders (UK)	charts coast of Australia and Bass Strait, circumnavigates Tasmania and explores the south coast of Australia
1807	John Colter (USA)	explores the region now known as Yellowstone National Park
1823	Hugh Clapperyon (UK)	reaches Lake Chad

Year	Explorer	Expedition
1829–30	Charles Sturt (Australia)	traces several rivers, including the River Murray
1841	John Fremont (USA)	leads expedition to River Des Moines, surveys the route to Wyoming, discovers the mouth of River Columbus and reaches California
1844–6	Charles Sturt (UK)	leads expedition from Adelaide to the Simpson Desert
1851–3	David Livingstone (UK)	reaches the Zambesi and in 1853 reaches Luanda
1853	Sir Richard Burton (UK)	reaches Mecca
1854	Sir Richard Burton	explores the interior of Somalia and reaches Harar in Ethiopia
1855	David Livingstone	follows the River Zambesi and discovers the Victoria Falls
1858–62	John Sturt	leads expeditions into the interior of Australia and reaches Van Diemen's Land
1858	Sir Richard Burton, John Speke (UK)	discovers Lake Tanganyika
1858	John Speke	reaches Lake Victoria and identifies it as the source of the River Nile

Year	Explorer	Expedition
1866–71	David Livingstone (UK)	explores country between Lake Nyasa and Lake Tanganyika, reaches Ujiji where Sir Henry Stanley meets him in 1871, together they explore northern Tanganyika
1869	Sir John Forest (Australia)	explores Western Australia
1873–7	Pierre de Brazza (It)	explores equatorial Africa
1874	Sir Henry Stanley (UK, USA)	crosses Africa from Zanzibar to the mouth of the River Congo
1897–8	Jean-Baptiste Marchand (Fr)	explores Africa from Libreville in Gabon to the Upper Nile
1909	Dr Frederick Cook (USA)	reaches the North Pole (disputed)
1909	Robert Peary (USA)	reaches the North Pole (disputed)
1911	Roald Amundsen (Nor)	reaches the South Pole

World Currencies

Money is any kind of commodity that serves as a common means of exchange and which is accepted by the community within which it circulates. A special sort of shell, for instance, has served as money on a Pacific island. However, when we speak of money today we think of coins and notes, and these are in use throughout the world.

Money Used

Country	Monetary Unit
Afghanistan	1 afghani = 100 puls
Albania	1 lek = 100 quindarka
Algeria	1 dinar = 100 centimes
Angola	1 kwanza = 100 lweis
Argentina	1 austral = 100 centavos
Australia	1 dollar = 100 cents
Austria	1 schilling = 100 groschen
Bahamas	1 dollar = 100 cents
Bahrain	1 dinar = 1,000 fils
Bangladesh	1 taka = 100 poisha
Barbados	1 dollar = 100 cents
Belgium	1 franc = 100 centimes
Belize	1 dollar = 100 cents
Benin	franc (CFA)
Bermuda	1 dollar = 100 cents
Bolivia	1 peso = 100 centavos
Botswana	1 pula = 100 thebe
Brazil	1 cruzeiro = 100 centavos
Brunei	1 dollar = 100 sen
Burkina Faso	franc (CFA)
Bulgaria	1 lev = 100 stotinki
Burma	1 kyat = 100 pyas
Burundi	franc
Cameroon	franc (CFA)
Canada	1 dollar = 100 cents
Cape Verde Islands	1 escudo = 100 centavos
Cayman Islands	1 dollar = 100 cents
Central African Republic	franc (CFA)
Chad	franc (CFA)
Chile	1 new peso = 100 centavos

Country	Monetary Unit
China	1 renminbi (or yuan) = 100 fen
Colombia	1 peso = 100 centavos
Congo	franc (CFA)
Costa Rica	1 colon = 100 céntimos
Cuba	1 peso = 100 centavos
Cyprus	1 pound = 1,000 mils
Czechoslovakia	1 koruna = 1 haléru
Denmark	1 krone = 100 ore
Domincan Republic	1 peso = 100 centavos
East Caribbean territory	1 dollar = 100 cents
Ecuador	1 sucre = 100 centavos
Egypt	1 pound = 100 piastres
El Salvador	1 colon = 100 centavos
Equatorial Guinea	ekuele
Ethiopia	1 birr = 100 cents
Falkland Islands	1 pound = 100 pence
Faroe Islands	1 krone = 100 ore
Fiji	1 dollar = 100 cents
Finland	1 markka = 100 penniä
France	1 franc = 100 centimes
Gabon	franc (CFA)
Gambia	1 dalasi = 100 bututs
Germany, East	1 mark = 100 pfennigs
Germany, West	1 Deutsche mark = 100 pfennigs
Ghana	1 cedi = 100 pesewa
Gibraltar	1 pound = 100 pence
Greece	1 drachma = 100 lepta
Guatemala	1 quetzal = 100 centavos
Guinea	1 syli = 100 cauris
Guinea-Bissau	1 escudos = 100 centavos
Guyana	1 dollar = 100 cents
Haiti	1 gourde = 100 centimes
Honduras	1 lempira = 100 centavos
Hong Kong	1 dollar = 100 cents
Hungary	1 forint = 100 fillér
Iceland	1 króna = 100 aurar
India	1 rupee = 100 paise
Indonesia	1 rupiah = 100 sen
Iran	1 rial = 100 dinars
Iraq	1 dinar = 1,000 fils

Country	Monetary Unit
Irish Republic	1 pound = 100 pence
Israel	1 shekel = 100 new agora
Italy	1 lira = 100 centesimi
Ivory Coast	franc (CFA)
Jamaica	1 dollar = 100 cents
Japan	yen
Jordan	1 dinar = 1,000 fils
Kenya	1 shilling = 100 cents
Korea, North	1 won = 100 chon
Korea, South	1 won = 100 jeon
Kuwait	1 dollar = 1,000 fils
Laos	1 kip = 100 ats
Lebanon	1 pound = 100 piastres
Liberia	1 dollar = 100 cents
Libya	1 dinar = 1,000 dirhams
Luxemburg	1 franc = 100 centimes
Macau	1 pataca = 100 avos
Malagsy Republic	franc Malgache (FMG)
Malawi	1 kwacha = 100 tambala
Malaysia	1 dollar (ringgit) = 100 cents
Maldive Islands	1 rufiyaa = 100 laris
Mali	franc (CFA)
Malta	1 pound = 100 cents
Mauritania	1 ouguiya = 5 khoums
Mauritius	1 rupee = 100 cents
Mexico	1 peso = 100 centavos
Monaco	1 franc = 100 centimes
Mongolian People's Republic	1 tugrik = 100 mongo
Morocco	1 dirham = 100 centimes
Mozambique	1 metical = 100 centavos
Nepal	1 rupee = 100 paisa
Netherlands	1 florin (guilder) = 100 cents
Netherlands Antilles	1 guilder = 100 cents
New Zealand	1 dollar = 100 cents
Nicaragua	1 córdoba = 100 centavos
Niger	franc (CFA)
Nigeria	1 naira = 100 kobo
Norway	1 krone = 100 ore
Oman	1 rial = 1,000 baiza
Pakistan	1 rupee = 100 paisa

Country	Monetary Unit
Panama	1 balboa = 100 cents
Papua New Guinea	1 kina = 100 toea
Paraguay	1 guarani = 100 céntimos
Peru	1 gold sol = 100 centavos
Philippines	1 peso = 100 centavos
Poland	1 zloty = 100 groszy
Portugal	1 escudo = 100 centavos
Portuguese Timor	1 escudo = 100 centavos
Qatar	1 riyal = 100 dirhams
Romania	1 leu = 100 bani
Rwanda	franc
St Helena	1 pound = 100 pence
Samoa, Western	1 tala = 100 sene
Sao Tome & Principe	1 dobra = 100 centimos
Saudi Arabia	1 riyal = 20 qursh or 100 halalas
Senegal	franc (FCA)
Seychelles	1 rupee = 100 cents
Sierra Leone	1 leone = 100 cents
Singapore	1 dollar = 100 cents
Solomon Islands	1 dollar = 100 cents
Somalia	1 shilling = 100 cents
South Africa	1 rand = 100 cents
Spain	1 peseta = 100 centimos
Sri Lanka	1 rupee = 100 cents
Sudan	1 pound = 100 piastres
Surinam	1 guilder = 100 cents
Swaziland	1 lilangeni = 100 cents
Sweden	1 krona = 100 ore
Switzerland	1 franc = 100 centimes
Syria	1 pound = 100 piastres
Taiwan	1 dollar = 100 cents
Tanzania	1 shilling = 100 cents
Thailand	1 baht = 100 stangs
Togo	franc (CFA)
Tonga	1 pa'anga = 100 seniti
Trinidad and Tobago	1 dollar = 100 cents
Tunisia	1 dinar = 1,000 millimes
Turkey	1 lira = 100 kurus
Uganda	1 shilling = 100 cents
United Arab Emirates	1 dirham = 100 fils

Country	Monetary Unit
UK	1 pound = 100 pence
USA	1 dollar = 100 cents
USSR	1 rouble = 100 copecks
Uruguay	1 new peso = 100 centésimos
Venezuela	bolivar
Vietnam	1 dông = 10 hào or 100 xu
Yemen Arab Republic	1 riyal = 100 fils
Yemen, People's Democratic Republic	1 dinar = 1,000 fils
Yugoslavia	1 dinar = 100 paras
Zaire	1 zaire = 100 makuta or 10,000 senghi
Zambia	1 kwacha = 100 ngwee
Zimbabwe	1 dollar = 100 cents

5 GOVERNMENT

Early government was despotic. The toughest, and therefore usually the most ruthless person, became the leader and he ruled as long as he was supported by the army. There are many countries in the world where this is still true today.

In Attica, in Greece, around 500 BC, everyone other than slaves had a right to elect members to the Council, and this democratic system of government was continued by Rome, although there were considerable modifications. However, after the fall of Rome and the end of its empire, it was a long time before the ordinary man had a say in government, although no king was able to rule without the support of powerful nobles.

The oldest legislative body in the world is the Althing in Iceland which was constituted in AD 930. It was abolished in 1800 and later restored. The legislative body with the longest *continuous* history is the Tynwald Court of the Isle of Man which was established over 1,000 years ago.

Hereditary Rulers: Monarchies, Principalities, etc.

Country	Ruler	Born	Succeeded
Bahrain	Amir H.H. Sheikh Isa bin Sulman Al Khalifa	1932	1961
Belgium	H.M. King Baudouin	1930	1951
Bhutan	H.M. King Jigme Singye Wangchuck	1955	1972
Denmark	H.M. Queen Margrethe II	1940	1972
Japan	H.M. Emperor Hirohito	1901	1926
Jordan	H.M. King Hussein	1935	1952
Kuwait	Amir H.M. Sheikh Jaber Al Ahmad Al Sabah	1928	1978
Liechtenstein	H.H. Prince Franz Josef II	1906	1938
Luxemburg	H.R.H. Grand Duke Jean	1921	1953
Monaco	H.S.H. Prince Rainier III	1923	1949
Morocco	H.M. King Hassan II	1929	1961
Nepal	H.M. King Birendra Bir Bikram Shah Dev	1945	1972

Country	Ruler	Born	Succeeded
Netherlands	H.M. Queen Beatrix Wilhemina	1938	1980
Norway	H.M. King Olav V	1903	1957
Qatar	Amir H.H. Sheikh Khalifa Bin Hamad Al-Thani	?	1972
Saudi Arabia	H.M. King Fahd bin Abdul Aziz	1921	1982
Spain	H.M. King Juan Carlos I	1938	1973
Sweden	H.M. King Carl XVI Gustaf	1946	1973
Thailand	H.M. Bhumibol Adulyadej	1927	1946
UK	H.R.H. Queen Elizabeth II	1926	1952
	(Head of State) Antigua and Barbuda; Australia; Bahamas; Barbados; Belize; Canada; Fiji; Grenada; Jamaica; Mauritius; New Zealand; Papua New Guinea; St Kitts-Nevis; St Lucia; St Vincent and Grenadines; Solomon Islands; Tuvalu; UK		

English Kings and Queens

When the Romans left Britain in the fourth and fifth centuries, there was mass invasion of the country by Germanic tribes. Eventually, Saxon kings ruled over parts of the country, battling against each other when they were not fighting off new invaders, and it wasn't until 829 that the country was united under Egbert, King of Wessex. There was constant trouble with the Danes, and in 1016 Canute, King of Denmark and Norway, became King of England; but it was only another twenty-six years before there was a Saxon king on the throne again.

Some of the dates, ages and causes of death of earlier kings are uncertain.

Name	Reigned	Age at Death	Cause of Death
Saxon and Danes			
Edgar	959–75	32	
Edward the Martyr	975–8	17	murdered
Ethelred	978–1016	48	
Edmund Ironside	1016	27	

Name	Reigned	Age at Death	Cause of Death
Canute	1017–35	40	natural
Harold I	1035–40		
Hardicanute	1040–2	24	natural
Edward the Confessor	1042–66	62	natural
Harold II	1066	44	killed in battle

Norman

William I	1066–87	60	result of accident
William II	1087–1100	43	uncertain, killed while hunting
Henry I	1100–35	67	natural
Stephen	1135–54	50	natural

Plantagenet

Henry II	1154–89	56	natural
Richard I	1189–99	42	killed in battle
John	1199–1216	50	natural
Henry III	1216–72	65	natural
Edward I	1272–1307	68	natural
Edward II	1307–27	43	murdered
Edward III	1327–77	65	natural
Richard II	1377–99 deposed	34	uncertain, believed murdered

Lancaster

Henry IV	1399–1413	47	natural
Henry V	1413–22	34	natural
Henry VI	1422–61 deposed		
	restored 1470–71 deposed	49	murdered

York

Edward IV	1461–70 deposed		
	restored 1471–83	41	natural
Edward V	1483	13	uncertain, believed murdered
Richard III	1483–85	32	killed in battle during rebellion

Name	Reigned	Age at Death	Cause of Death
Tudor			
Henry VII	1485–1509	53	natural
Henry VIII	1509–47	56	natural
Edward VI	1547–53	16	natural
Jane	1553	17	executed 1554
Mary I	1553–58	43	natural
Elizabeth I	1558–1603	69	natural
Stuart			
James I	1603–25	59	natural
(VI of Scotland)			
Charles I	1625–49	48	executed
Commonwealth	1649–60		
Charles II	1660–85	55	natural
James II	1685–88 deposed	68	natural
William III and	1688–1702	51	natural
Mary II	1688–94	33	natural
Anne	1702–14	49	natural
Hanover			
George I	1714–27	67	natural
George II	1727–60	77	natural
George III	1760–1820	81	natural
George IV	1820–30	67	natural
William IV	1830–37	71	natural
Victoria	1837–1901	81	natural
Saxe-Coburg			
Edward VII	1901–10	68	natural
Windsor			
George V	1910–36	70	natural
Edward VIII	1936 abdicated	77	natural
George VI	1937–52	56	natural
Elizabeth II	1952		

Scottish Kings and Queens

(from unification of Scotland–unification with England)

Name	Reigned
Celtic	
Malcolm II	1005–34
Duncan I	1034–40
Macbeth	1040–57
Malcolm III Canmore	1057–93
Donald Ban	1093–4 deposed
Duncan II	1094–5
Donald Ban restored	1095–7
Edgar	1097–1107
Alexander I	1107–24
David I	1124–53
Malcolm IV	1153–65
William the Lion	1165–1214
Alexander II	1214–49
Alexander III	1249–86
Margaret, the Maid of Norway	1286–90
English Domination	
John Baliol	1292–96
	1296–1306 annexed to England
Bruce	
Robert I (Bruce)	1306–29
David II	1329–71
Stuart	
Robert II	1371–90
Robert III	1390–1406
James I	1406–37
James II	1437–60
James III	1460–88
James IV	1488–1513
James V	1513–42
Mary	1542–67
James VI	1567
	1603 union of crowns

Presidents of the USA

Presidents of the USA are elected for a four-year term, but may stand for re-election for a second term. An exception was made in the case of Franklin Delano Roosevelt, who was re-elected for a third term in 1944.

Name	Inaug.	Life Span	Party
George Washington	1789	1732–99	Federalist
John Adams	1797	1735–1826	Federalist
Thomas Jefferson	1801	1743–1826	Republican
James Madison	1809	1751–1836	Republican
James Monroe	1817	1758–1831	Republican
John Quincy Adams	1825	1767–1848	Republican
Andrew Jackson	1829	1767–1845	Democrat
Martin Van Buren	1837	1782–1862	Democrat
William Henry Harrison	1841	1773–1841 died in office	Whig
John Tyler	1841	1790–1862	Whig
James Knox Polk	1845	1795–1849	Democrat
Zachary Taylor	1849	1784–1850 died in office	Whig
Millard Fillmore	1850	1800–74	Whig
Franklin Pierce	1853	1804–69	Democrat
James Buchanan	1857	1791–1868	Democrat
Abraham Lincoln	1861	1809–65 assassinated	Republican
Andrew Johnson	1865	1808–75	Republican
Ulysses Simpson Grant	1869	1822–85	Republican
Rutherford Birchard Hayes	1877	1822–93	Republican
James Abram Garfield	1881	1831–81 assassinated	Republican
Chester Alan Arthur	1881	1830–86	Republican
Grover Cleveland	1885	1837–1908	Democrat
Benjamin Harrison	1889	1833–1901	Republican
Grover Cleveland	1893	1837–1908	Democrat
Wiliam McKinley	1897	1843–1901 assassinated	Republican
Theodore Roosevelt	1901	1858–1919	Republican
William Howard Taft	1909	1857–1930	Republican

Name	Inaug.	Life Span	Party
Woodrow Wilson	1913	1856–1924	Democrat
Warren Gamaliel Harding	1921	1865–1923 died in office	Republican
Calvin Coolidge	1923	1872–1933	Republican
Herbert Clark Hoover	1929	1874–1964	Republican
Franklin Delano Roosevelt	1933	1882–1945 died in office	Democrat
Harry S. Truman	1945	1884–1972	Democrat
Dwight David Eisenhower	1953	1890–1969	Republican
John Fitzgerald Kennedy	1961	1917–63 assassinated	Democrat
Lyndon Baines Johnson	1963	1908–1973	Democrat
Richard Milhous Nixon	1969	1913	Republican
Gerald Rudolph Ford	1974	1913	Republican
James Earl Carter	1977	1924	Democrat
Ronald Wilson Reagan	1981	1911	Republican

Systems of Government Today

Country	Military	One Party	Parliamentary	Restricted Parliamentary
Afghanistan	★			
Albania		★		
Algeria			★	
Angola		★		
Antigua and Barbuda			★	

Country	Military	One Party	Parliamentary	Restricted Parliamentary
Argentina			★	
Australia			★	
Austria			★	
Bahamas			★	
Bangladesh	★			
Barbados			★	
Belgium			★	
Belize			★	
Benin	★			
Bermuda			★	
Bolivia			★	
Botswana			★	
Brazil			★	
Bulgaria		★		
Burkina Faso	★			
Burma		★		
Cameroon			★	
Canada			★	
Cape Verde Islands		★		
Central African Republic	★			

Country	Military	One Party	Parliamentary	Restricted Parliamentary
Chad		★		
Chile	★			
China		★		
Colombia			★	
Congo		★		
Costa Rica			★	
Cuba		★		
Cyprus			★	
Czechoslovakia		★		
Denmark			★	
Dominica			★	
Dominican Republic			★	
Ecuador			★	
Egypt			★	
El Salvador			★	
Ethiopia	★			
Falkland Islands			★	
Fiji			★	
Finland			★	
France			★	

Country	Military	One Party	Parliamentary	Restricted Parliamentary
Gabon		★		
Gambia			★	
Germany, East		★		
Germany, West			★	
Ghana	★			
Gibraltar			★	
Greece			★	
Grenada			★	
Guatemala	★			
Guinea	★			
Guinea-Bissau				★
Guyana			★	
Haiti	★			
Honduras			★	
Hungary		★		
Iceland			★	
India			★	
Indonesia			★	
Irish Republic			★	
Israel			★	

Country	Military	One Party	Parliamentary	Restricted Parliamentary
Iran		★		
Iraq		★		
Italy			★	
Ivory Coast			★	
Jamaica			★	
Japan			★	
Jordan			★	
Kampuchea		★		
Kenya		★		
Kiribati			★	
Korea, North		★		
Korea, South			★	
Laos		★		
Lesotho	★			
Lebanon				★
Liberia	★			
Libya		★		
Liechtenstein			★	
Luxemburg			★	
Madagascar				★

Country	Military	One Party	Parliamentary	Restricted Parliamentary
Malawi		★		
Malaysia			★	
Maldives			★	
Mali			★	
Malta			★	
Mauritania			★	
Mauritius			★	
Mexico			★	
Mongolia		★		
Montserrat			★	
Morocco			★	
Mozambique		★		
Nauru			★	
Netherlands			★	
New Zealand			★	
Nicaragua		★		
Niger	★			
Nigeria	★			
Norway			★	
Pakistan	★			

Country	Military	One Party	Parliamentary	Restricted Parliamentary
Papua New Guinea			★	
Paraguay			★	
Peru			★	
Philippines			★	
Poland		★		
Portugal			★	
Romania		★		
Rwanda	★			
St Kitts-Nevis			★	
St Lucia			★	
St Vincent and Grenadines			★	
San Marino			★	
São Tomé and Principe			★	
Senegal			★	
Seychelles		★		
Sierra Leone		★		
Singapore			★	
Somalia			★	
South Africa				★
Spain			★	

Country	Military	One Party	Parliamentary	Restricted Parliamentary
Sri Lanka			★	
Sudan				★
Surinam	★			
Sweden			★	
Switzerland			★	
Syria			★	
Tanzania		★		
Thailand			★	
Togo	★			
Trinidad and Tobago			★	
Turkey			★	
Tuvalu			★	
Uganda	★			
UK			★	
USA			★	
USSR		★		
Uruguay			★	
Vanuata			★	
Venezuela			★	
Vietnam		★		

Country	Military	One Party	Parliamentary	Restricted Parliamentary
Yugoslavia		★		
Zaire	★			
Zambia		★		
Zimbabwe			★	

International Organizations

Many international organizations have been established since the end of the Second World War. Some are listed below.
United Nations (UN) 1945
European Economic Community (EEC) 1958
Commonwealth (C) 1931 as British Commonwealth of Nations
Council for Mutual Economic Assistance (COMECON) 1949
Arab League (AL) 1945
North Atlantic Treaty Organization (NATO) 1949
Organization of American States (OAS) 1890
Organization for Economic Cooperation and Development (OECD) 1961
Caribbean Community and Common Market (CARICOM) 1973

Country	UN	EEC	C	COMECON	AL	NATO	OAS	OECD	CARICOM
Afghanistan	★								
Albania	★								
Algeria	★				★				
Angola	★								
Antigua and Barbuda	★		★				★		★
Argentina	★						★		

Country	UN	EEC	C	COMECON	AL	NATO	OAS	OECD	CARICOM
Australia	★		★					★	
Austria	★							★	
Bahamas	★		★				★		★
Bahrain	★				★				
Bangladesh	★		★						
Barbados	★		★				★		★
Belgium	★	★				★		★	
Belize	★		★						★
Benin	★								
Bhutan	★								
Bolivia	★						★		
Botswana	★		★						
Brazil	★						★		
Brunei	★		★						
Bulgaria	★			★					
Burkina Faso	★								
Burma	★								
Burundi	★								
Cameroon	★								
Canada	★		★			★		★	

138

Country	UN	EEC	C	COMECON	AL	NATO	OAS	OECD	CARICOM
Cape Verde Islands	★								
Central African Republic	★								
Chad	★								
Chile	★						★		
China	★								
Colombia	★						★		
Comoros	★								
Congo	★								
Costa Rica	★						★		
Cuba	★			★			★		
Cyprus	★		★						
Czechoslovakia	★			★					
Denmark	★	★				★		★	
Djibouti	★				★				
Dominica	★		★				★		★
Dominican Republic	★						★		
Ecuador	★						★		
Egypt	★								

139

Country	UN	EEC	C	COMECON	AL	NATO	OAS	OECD	CARICOM
El Salvador	★						★		
Equatorial Guinea	★								
Ethiopia	★								
Fiji	★		★						
Finland	★							★	
France	★	★				★		★	
Gabon	★								
Gambia	★		★						
Germany, East	★			★					
Germany, West	★	★				★		★	
Ghana	★		★						
Greece	★	★				★		★	
Grenada	★		★				★		★
Guatemala	★						★		
Guinea	★								
Guinea-Bissau	★								
Guyana	★		★				★		★
Haiti	★						★		
Honduras	★						★		

Country	UN	EEC	C	COMECON	AL	NATO	OAS	OECD	CARICOM
Hungary	★			★					
Iceland	★					★		★	
India	★		★						
Indonesia	★								
Iran	★								
Iraq	★				★				
Irish Republic	★	★						★	
Israel	★								
Italy	★	★				★		★	
Ivory Coast	★								
Jamaica	★		★				★		★
Japan	★							★	
Jordan	★				★				
Kampuchea	★								
Kenya	★		★						
Kiribati			★						
Kuwait	★				★				
Laos	★								
Lebanon	★				★				
Lesotho	★		★						

Country	UN	EEC	C	COMECON	AL	NATO	OAS	OECD	CARICOM
Liberia	★								
Libya	★				★				
Luxemburg	★	★				★		★	
Madagascar	★								
Malawi	★		★						
Malaysia	★		★						
Maldives	★		★						
Mali	★								
Malta	★		★						
Mauritania	★				★				
Mauritius	★		★						
Mexico	★						★		
Mongolia	★			★					
Morocco	★				★				
Mozambique	★								
Nauru			★						
Nepal	★								
Netherlands	★	★				★		★	
New Zealand	★		★					★	
Nicaragua	★						★		

Country	UN	EEC	C	COMECON	AL	NATO	OAS	OECD	CARICOM
Nigeria	★		★						
Norway	★					★		★	
Oman	★				★				
Pakistan	★								
Panama	★						★		
Papua New Guinea	★		★						
Paraguay	★						★		
Peru	★						★		
Philippines	★								
Poland	★			★					
Portugal	★	★				★		★	
Qatar	★				★				
Romania	★			★					
Rwanda	★								
St Kitts-Nevis	★		★				★		★
St Lucia	★		★				★		★
St Vincent and Grenadines	★		★				★		★
São Tomé and Principe	★								

Country	UN	EEC	C	COMECON	AL	NATO	OAS	OECD	CARICOM
Saudi Arabia	★				★				
Senegal	★								
Seychelles	★		★						
Sierra Leone	★		★						
Singapore	★		★						
Solomon Islands	★		★						
Somalia	★				★				
South Africa	★								
Spain	★	★				★		★	
Sri Lanka	★		★						
Sudan	★				★				
Surinam	★						★		
Swaziland	★		★						
Sweden	★							★	
Switzerland								★	
Tanzania	★		★						
Thailand	★								
Togo	★								

Country	UN	EEC	C	COMECON	AL	NATO	OAS	OECD	CARICOM
Tonga			★						
Trinidad and Tobago	★		★				★		★
Tunisia	★				★				
Turkey	★					★		★	
Tuvalu			★						
Uganda	★		★						
United Arab Emirates	★				★				
UK	★	★	★			★		★	
USA	★					★	★	★	
USSR	★			★					
Uruguay	★						★		
Vanuata	★		★						
Venezuela	★						★		
Vietnam	★			★					
Western Samoa	★		★						
Yemen, North	★				★				
Yemen, South	★				★				

Country	UN	EEC	C	COMECON	AL	NATO	OAS	OECD	CARICOM
Yugoslavia	★		★						
Zaire	★								
Zambia	★		★						
Zimbabwe	★		★						

Other International Organizations

Members

Association of South-East Asian Nations (ASEAN)	Brunei, Indonesia, Malaysia, Philippines, Singapore, Thailand
European Free Trade Association (EFTA)	Austria, Iceland, Norway, Portugal, Sweden, Switzerland, Finland (Associate)

United Nations

Secretary-General: Javier Perez de Cuellar (Peru)

On 26 June 1945, the fifty founder nations signed the Charter of the United Nations.

General Assembly consists of member states of the UN. Although each country may have up to five representatives, it has only one vote.

Security Council consists of fifteen members. The five permanent members are China, France, UK, USA, and the USSR. The other ten members are elected and serve a two-year term.

International Court of Justice, based in The Hague, consists of fifteen judges, each from a different country.

Agencies of the United Nations

FAO	Food and Agriculture Organization
IBRD	International Bank for Reconstruction and Development
ICAO	International Civil Aviation Organization
IDA	International Development Organization

IFAD	International Fund for Agricultural Development
IFC	International Finance Corporation
ILO	International Labour Organization
IMF	International Monetary Fund
IMO	International Maritime Organization
ITU	International Telecomunication Union
UNESCO	United Nations Education, Scientific and Cultural Organization
UPU	Universal Postal Union
WHO	World Health Organization
WIPO	World Intellectual Property Organization
WMO	World Meteorological Organization

Flags

Flags have been around for thousands of years. They were in use in Ancient Egypt and during early Mesopotamian and Chinese civilizations, but they didn't flutter in the breeze. They were solid objects mounted on poles and sometimes adorned with strips of coloured cloth.

It wasn't until the rise of Islam that banners with designs on cloth, usually inscriptions, were seen, and the idea was taken up by Christians. At first they used a simple cross, but later the emblems became more complex.

Terminology of Flags

1 hoist	the vertical half of the flag nearest the staff or flagpole
2 fly	the outer half of the flag
3 cantons	the four quarters of the flag
4 the canton	the upper hoist canton, i.e., the quarter at the top nearest the staff

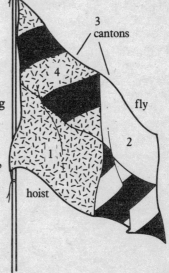

Some Flags of the World

Country	Date Adopted	Description
Australia	1901	blue flag with the Union Jack in the upper hoist canton; beneath the Union Jack a large white star representing Australia, five other smaller white stars representing the Southern Cross
Belgium	1789	three vertical bands; black next to the staff, yellow and red
Canada	1965	red maple leaf with eleven points on central white background with vertical red bars, one half the width of the maple leaf, on either side
China	1949	a red flag, as used by all communist countries, with a gold star near the staff and four gold stars round it in a crescent representing the peasants, the workers, the petty bourgeoisie and patriotic capitalists
Cyprus	1960	white flag with a yellow map of the island; two olive branches beneath the map
Denmark	1219	red with white cross, the vertical being closer to the staff
Egypt	1970	horizontal bands of red, white and black with an eagle in the centre of the white band; the scroll grasped by the eagle reads 'Egyptian Arab Republic'
England	1277	red cross of St George on a white background; traditionally flown on 23 April
France	1794	the tricolour: red, white and blue vertical stripes, the blue being closest to the staff

Country	Date Adopted	Description
Germany, West	1949	horizontal bars of black, red and gold
India	1947	horizontal bands of deep saffron, white and dark green with the deep blue Buddhist symbol of the chakra; the colours represent Hindus and Moslems
Irish Republic	1848	vertical stripes of green, white and orange, the green being nearest the staff; Protestants are represented by orange, Catholics by green
Israel	1948	white flag with two horizontal blue bands close to the top and bottom, a white central band with the blue Star of David in the middle
Jamaica	1962	gold diagonal cross forming triangles of green at the top and bottom with triangles of black nearest the staff and opposite
Netherlands	1650	horizontal bands of red, white and blue; at one time the red was orange
New Zealand	1869	blue with Union Jack in upper hoist canton, four five-pointed red stars edged in white representing the Southern Cross
Norway	1821	red with white bordered blue cross, the vertical stripe being closer to the staff
Northern Ireland	1953	red cross on a white background, a white star representing the six counties with the red hand of the O'Neills in the centre of the star, a crown above the star
Pakistan	1947	dark green representing Moslems, a white vertical stripe at the

Country	Date Adopted	Description
		staff for non-Moslems, a white crescent in the centre and a five-pointed star on the green
Scotland	uncertain, pre-dates England	white diagonal cross of St Andrew on a blue background
UK	1801	Union Jack: a combination of flags representing England, Scotland and Ireland; the broad white band of the cross of St Andrew is above the red band of the cross of St Patrick in the upper hoist canton
USA	evolved since 1775	Stars and Stripes: seven red and six white equidistant horizontal stripes, upper hoist canton blue with fifty white stars representing the number of states in the union
USSR	1923	red flag with gold hammer and sickle representing workers and peasants in the upper hoist canton near the staff, and just below a small gold star
Wales	1959	horizontal stripes of red and green, a red dragon straddling both stripes

International Flags

Organization	Adopted	Description
International Red Cross	1869	red cross on a white background
Council of Europe	1953	blue with a circle of twelve gold stars in the centre
NATO	1953	blue background with a white compass rose within a circle and with four rays

Organization	Adopted	Description
Olympic Games	1913	white flag with interlaced circles of blue, gold, black, green and red representing the five continents
United Nations	1947	mid-blue flag with central UN emblem in white, a map of the world projected from above the north pole and surrounded by olive branches

Some Naval Flags

Blue Ensign	flag with dark-blue background and the Union Jack in the upper hoist canton; flown by ships in government service
Red Ensign	flag with red background and the Union Jack in the upper hoist canton; flown by British merchant ships, sometimes called the Red Duster
White Ensign	flag with white background and the Union Jack in the upper hoist canton; flown by ships of the Royal Navy; the Royal Yacht Squadron may also fly this flag

---

Some International Airlines

Country	Airlines	Distance to London	(km)
Algeria	Air Algérie	Algiers	1,666
Australia	QANTAS	Brisbane	16,532
		Darwin	13,861
		Sydney	17,007
Austria	Austrian Airlines	Salzburg	1,049
		Vienna	1,271
Belgium	SABENA	Brussels	349
Bulgaria	Bulgarian Airlines	Sofia	2,037
Canada	Air Canada	Montreal	5,215
		Toronto	5,681
Cyprus	Cyprus Airways	Larnaca	3,277
Czechoslovakia	Czechoslovak Airlines	Prague	1,045

Country	Airlines	Distance to London	(km)
Denmark	SAS	Copenhagen	978
Egypt	Egyptair	Cairo	3,534
Finland	Finnair	Helsinki	1,845
France	Air France	Nice	1,038
		Paris	346
Germany, East	Interflug	Berlin	947
Germany, West	Lufthansa	Cologne	532
		Hamburg	745
Greece	Olympic Airways	Athens	2,414
Hong Kong	Cathay Pacific Airways	Hong Kong	9,640
Hungary	Malév	Budapest	1,485
India	Air India	Bombay	7,206
		Calcutta	7,979
		Delhi	6,726
Iran	Iranair	Teheran	4,410
Iraq	Iraqi Airways	Baghdad	4,105
Irish Republic	Aer Lingus	Dublin	448
Israel	El Al	Tel Aviv	3,586
Italy	Alitalia	Naples	1,627
		Rome	1,440
Jamaica	Air Jamaica	Kingston	7,512
Japan	Japan Air Lines	Tokyo	16,022
Kenya	Kenya Airways	Nairobi	6,834
Kuwait	Kuwait Airways	Kuwait	4,672
Lebanon	MEA	Beirut	3,478
Libya	Libyan Arab Airlines	Tripoli	2,362
Malaysia	Air Malaysia	Kuala Lumpur	10,552
Malta	Air Malta	Valletta	2,090
Morocco	Royal Air Maroc	Tangier	1,802
Netherlands	KLM	Amsterdam	370
New Zealand	Air New Zealand	Auckland	18,352
Norway	SAS	Oslo	1,164
Poland	LOT	Warsaw	1,468
Portugal	TAP	Lisbon	1,564
		Oporto	1,297
Singapore	Singapore Airlines	Singapore	10,872
South Africa	South African Airlines	Johannesburg	9,063
Spain	Iberia	Barcelona	1,147
		Madrid	1,243

Country	Airlines	Distance to London	(km)
Sudan	Sudan Airways	Khartoum	4,942
Sweden	SAS	Stockholm	1,461
Switzerland	Swissair	Geneva	754
Thailand	Thai Airways International	Bangkok	9,540
Trinidad and Tobago	BWIA International	Port of Spain	7,089
Turkey	THY	Ankara	2,848
		Istanbul	2,510
USA	Air Florida	Chicago	6,342
	Delta	Detroit	5,941
	Northwest Orient	New York	5,526
	PanAm		
	TWA		
	World		
USSR	Aeroflot	Leningrad	2,114
		Moscow	2,508
Yugoslav	Yugoslavia Airlines	Zagreb	1,364

6 THE WORLD'S RESOURCES

Growth of the World's Population

The population of the world is increasing at an alarming rate: 216,400 extra people have to be fed, clothed and housed each day. It has been estimated that if the population explosion continues at its present rate, by the year 2600 each person will have just over a square metre on which to live, and that by the year 3700 the total weight of the world's population will exceed that of the earth itself.

Year BC	Population
10,000	5,000,000

Year AD			
1	200,000,000	1900	1,550,000,000
1000	275,000,000	1925	2,500,000,000
1250	375,000,000	1960	3,003,000,000
1500	420,000,000	1975	3,967,000,000
1750	720,000,000	1985	4,684,000,000
1850	1,094,000,000	2000 (projected)	6,267,000,000

Africa

Country	Capital	Area (km²)	Population
Algeria	Algiers	2,381,000	20,200,000
Angola	Luanda	1,246,000	7,100,000
Benin	Porto Novo	115,000	3,338,000
Botswana	Gaborone	575,000	937,000
Burkina Faso	Ouagadougou	260,000	6,600,000
Burundi	Bujumbura	27,800	4,480,000
Cameroon	Yaoundé	475,000	8,320,000
Cape Verde Islands	Praia	4,030	296,000
Central African Republic	Bangui	625,000	2,347,000

Country	Capital	Area (km^2)	Population
Chad	N'Djaména	1,284,000	4,000,000
Comoros	Moroni	1,900	385,000
Congo	Brazzaville	349,000	2,100,000
Djibouti	Djibouti	23,000	350,000
Egypt	Cairo	1,000,250	47,000,000
Equatorial Guinea	Malabo	28,000	300,000
Ethiopia	Addis Ababa	1,222,000	42,000,000
Gabon	Libreville	265,000	1,200,000
Gambia	Banjul	10,600	700,000
Ghana	Accra	238,000	12,206,000
Guinea	Conakry	245,800	6,412,000
Guinea Bissau	Bissau	36,125	920,000
Ivory Coast	Abidjan	320,000	9,924,000
Kenya	Nairobi	582,600	17,000,000
Lesotho	Maseru	30,340	1,205,000
Liberia	Monrovia	112,000	2,110,000
Libya	Tripoli	1,760,000	3,100,000
Madagascar	Antananarivo	590,000	9,230,000
Malawai	Lilongwe	94,485	6,270,000
Mali	Bamako	1,204,000	7,160,000
Mauritania	Nouakchott	1,118,000	1,634,000
Mauritius	Port Louis	1,865	1,000,000
Mayotte	Dzaoudzi	376	50,000
Morocco	Rabat	660,000	20,420,000
Mozambique	Maputo	784,000	12,600,000
Namibia	Windhoëk	824,300	1,040,000
Niger	Niamey	1,118,000	6,170,000
Nigeria	Lagos	923,000	85,000,000
Réunion	St Denis	2,510	518,000
Rwanda	Kigali	26,330	5,130,000
St Helena, Ascension, Tristan de Cunha	Jamestown	300	8,000
São Tomé, Principe	São Tomé	965	113,000
Senegal	Dakar	197,000	5,660,000
Seychelles	Victoria	405	65,000
Sierra Leone	Freetown	73,320	3,670,000
Somalia	Mogadishu	637,000	5,000,000
South Africa	Pretoria	1,175,000	31,000,000
Sudan	Khartoum	2,500,000	19,500,000

155

Country	Capital	Area (km^2)	Population
Swaziland	Mbabane	17,400	600,000
Tanzania	Dar-es-Salaam	945,000	17,550,000
Togo	Lomé	56,500	2,470,000
Tunisia	Tunis	164,150	6,960,000
Uganda	Kampala	236,000	12,600,000
Zaire	Kinshasha	2,345,000	29,400,000
Zambia	Lusaka	752,600	6,050,000
Zimbabwe	Harare	390,000	7,960,000

America: Central and West Indies

Country	Capital	Area (km^2)	Population
Anguilla	The Valley	91	7,000
Antigua and Barbuda	St John's	443	78,000
Bahamas	Nassau	11,500	237,000
Barbados	Bridgetown	431	249,000
Belize	Belmopan	22,965	148,000
British Virgin Islands	Road Town	153	12,000
Cayman Islands	George Town	260	19,000
Costa Rica	San José	50,900	2,277,000
Cuba	Havana	114,525	10,042,000
Dominica	Roseau	750	74,000
Dominican Republic	Santo Domingo	48,000	5,648,000
El Salvador	San Salvador	21,000	4,940,000
Grenada	St George's	345	110,000
Guadeloupe	Basse-Terre	1,780	328,000
Guatemala	Guatemala	108,890	7,932,000
Haiti	Port au Prince	27,750	6,009,000
Honduras	Tegucigalpa	112,090	3,600,000
Jamaica	Kingston	11,400	2,265,000
Martinique	Fort de France	1,100	328,000
Mexico	Mexico City	1,970,000	67,380,000
Montserrat	Plymouth	98	12,000
Netherland Antilles	Willemstad	1,000	253,000
Nicaragua	Managua	148,000	3,200,000
Panama	Panama City	75,650	1,940,000
Puerto Rico	San Juan	8,895	3,200,000

Country	Capital	Area (km^2)	Population
St Kitts–Nevis	Basseterre	300	44,500
St Lucia	Castries	616	134,000
St Vincent	Kingstown	389	128,000
Trinidad and Tobago	Port of Spain	5,128	1,056,000
Turks and Caicos Islands	Grand Turk	430	7,500
US Virgin Islands	Charlotte Amalie	345	96,000

America: North

Country	Capital	Area (km^2)	Population
Canada	Ottawa	9,976,140	25,320,000
Greenland	Godthab	2,175,600	52,000
Mexico	Mexico City	1,970,000	67,380,000
St Pierre and Miquelon	St Pierre	93	6,000
USA	Washington	9,363,000	231,000,000

America: South

Country	Capital	Area (km^2)	Population
Argentina	Buenos Aires	2,776,000	27,860,000
Bolivia	La Paz	1,098,580	6,000,000
Brazil	Brasilia	8,511,970	119,099,000
Chile	Santiago	750,000	11,000,000
Colombia	Bogotá	1,138,900	28,100,000
Ecuador	Quito	455,000	8,000,000
Falkland Islands	Stanley	11,950	1,800
French Guinea	Cayenne	90,000	73,000
Guyana	Georgetown	262,000	793,000
Paraguay	Ascensioń	406,750	3,475,000
Peru	Lima	1,285,000	18,790,000
Surinam	Paramaribo	163,500	410,000
Uruguay	Montevideo	186,925	3,012,000
Venezuela	Caracas	912,050	17,255,000

Asia

Country	Capital	Area (km^2)	Population
Afghanistan	Kabul	650,000	16,790,000
Bahrain	Manama	600	351,000
Bangladesh	Dhaka	142,750	94,700,000
Bhutan	Thimphu	47,000	1,300,000
Brunei	Bandar Seri Begawan	5,765	214,000
Burma	Rangoon	678,000	35,314,000
China	Peking	9,560,000	1,008,000,000
Christmas Island		140	3,300
Cocos Island	West Island	14	450
Hong Kong	Victoria	1,040	5,395,000
India	New Delhi	3,200,000	685,185,000
Indonesia	Jakarta	1,915,000	157,000,000
Iran	Tehran	1,648,000	42,000,000
Iraq	Baghdad	434,000	14,000,000
Israel	Jerusalem	20,700	4,148,000
Japan	Tokyo	370,000	118,390,000
Jordan	Amman	97,740	2,950,000
Kampuchea	Phnom Penh	181,000	6,000,000
Korea, North	Pyongyang	122,000	20,000,000
Korea, South	Seoul	98,000	42,000,000
Kuwait	Kuwait	24,000	1,786,000
Laos	Vientiane	236,000	3,900,000
Lebanon	Beirut	10,400	2,740,000
Macau	Macau	16	262,000
Malaysia	Kuala Lumpur	331,000	13,436,000
Maldive Islands	Malé	298	160,000
Mongolia	Ulan Bator	1,565,000	1,866,000
Nepal	Kathmandu	141,400	16,000,000
Oman	Muscat	212,400	850,000
Pakistan	Islamabad	800,000	83,780,000
Philippines	Manila	299,000	54,400,000
Qatar	Doha	10,750	250,000
Saudi Arabia	Riyadh	2,260,000	9,160,000
Singapore	Singapore	600	2,544,000
Sri Lanka	Colombo	65,610	14,800,000
Syria	Damascus	185,200	10,400,000

Country	Capital	Area (km²)	Population
Taiwan	Taipei	35,980	18,271,000
Thailand	Bangkok	514,000	50,583,000
Turkey	Ankara	780,575	45,218,000
United Arab Emirates	Abu Dhabi	86,400	1,300,000
USSR (see also Europe)	Moscow	16,704,000	60,000,000
Vietnam	Hanoi	330,000	60,000,000
Yemen Arab Republic	San'a	195,000	8,557,000
Yemen (People's Democratic Republic)	Aden	290,000	2,080,000

Europe

Country	Capital	Area (km²)	Population
Albania	Tirana	28,750	2,752,000
Andorra	Andorra La Vella	453	41,600
Austria	Vienna	83,850	7,551,000
Belgium	Brussels	30,500	9,863,000
Bulgaria	Sofia	110,900	8,929,000
Cyprus	Nicosia	9,250	650,000
Czechoslovakia	Prague	128,000	15,280,000
Denmark	Copenhagen	43,000	5,116,000
Finland	Helsinki	350,000	4,844,000
France	Paris	554,000	54,334,000
Germany, East (GDR)	East Berlin	108,000	16,740,000
Germany, West (FDR)	Bonn	248,600	61,050,000
Gibraltar	Gibraltar		628,700
Greece	Athens	132,000	9,740,000
Hungary	Budapest	93,000	10,710,000
Iceland	Reykjavik	102,800	238,000
Irish Republic	Dublin	70,300	3,444,000
Italy	Rome	301,220	57,080,000
Liechenstein	Vaduz	160	26,500
Luxemburg	Luxemburg	2,600	365,500

Country	Capital	Area (km^2)	Population
Malta	Valletta	316	341,000
Monaco	Monaco-ville	1.6	28,000
Netherlands	Amsterdam	36,000	14,395,000
Norway	Oslo	324,000	4,145,000
Poland	Warsaw	312,000	36,400,000
Portugal	Lisbon	91,750	10,030,000
Romania	Bucharest	237,500	22,480,000
San Marino	San Marino	60	22,000
Spain	Madrid	504,700	37,834,000
Sweden	Stockholm	500,000	8,330,000
Switzerland	Berne	41,285	6,482,000
United Kingdom	London	244,000	55,766,422
England	London	130,362	46,362,836
Northern Ireland	Belfast	14,147	1,491,000
Scotland	Edinburgh	78,749	5,130,735
Wales	Cardiff	20,761	2,791,851
USSR (see also Asia)	Moscow	5,568,000	214,397,000
Vatican City State	Vatican City	0.44	730
Yugoslavia	Belgrade	255,803	22,800,000

Oceania

Country	Capital	Area (km^2)	Population
American Samoa	Fagatogo	197	32,300
Australia	Canberra	7,686,000	15,452,000
Cook Islands	Avarua	241	17,500
Fiji	Suva	18,270	677,000
French Polynesia	Papeete	4,200	168,000
Kiribati	Tarawa	655	63,000
Guam	Agaña	549	106,000
Mariana, Caroline, Marshall Islands	Saipan	479	133,000
Nauru	Nauru	21	8,040
New Caledonia	Noumea	19,100	145,000
New Zealand	Wellington	268,700	3,265,000
Niue	Alofi	259	3,000
Norfolk Island	Kingston	35	1,600
Papua New Guinea	Port Moresby	461,690	3,160,000

Country	Capital	Area (km²)	Population
Pitcairn Islands	Adamstown	48	60
Solomon Islands	Honiara	29,785	244,000
Tonga	Nuku'alofa	700	98,000
Wallis and Futuna Islands	Mata-Utu	240	12,400
Western Samoa	Apia	28,421	158,130

The Top Ten Cities of the World

City	Country	Population
Mexico City	Mexico	16,000,000
Shanghai	China	11,859,000
Tokyo	Japan	11,807,000
Cairo	Egypt	11,500,000
Paris	France	10,073,000
Buenos Aires	Argentina	9,677,000
Peking	China	9,231,000
Calcutta	India	9,200,000
Moscow	USSR	8,537,000
São Paulo	Brazil	8,491,000

Some Other Cities

City	Country	Population
Amsterdam	Netherlands	687,397
Belfast	Northern Ireland	297,862
Bonn	West Germany	292,900
Brussels	Belgium	1,000,221
Canberra	Australia	281,300
Cardiff	Wales	279,800
Chicago	USA	3,005,072
Copenhagen	Denmark	575,217
Edinburgh	Scotland	446,361
Edmonton	Canada	682,000
London	England	6,696,008
Madrid	Spain	3,188,297
New York	USA	7,071,030
Oslo	Norway	448,747

City	Country	Population
Ottawa	Canada	756,600
Quebec	Canada	163,800
Stanley	Falkland Islands	1,050
Sydney	Australia	3,335,250
Washington DC	USA	633,425
Wellington	New Zealand	342,400

Channel Islands

Alderney	2,000
Guernsey	54,380
Jersey	76,050
Sark	604

Isle of Man

64,679

Scilly Islands

1,850

Isle of Wight

120,400

Densely Populated Territories

Country	Population (km^2)
Macau	21,805
Monaco	14,195
Hong Kong	4,988

Expectation of Life

Many factors, including climate, diet and medical facilities, affect life expectancy. In almost every country of the world, women can expect to live longer than men.

Countries with the Highest Expectation of Life

Men	Years	Women	Years
Iceland	74	Iceland	80
Japan, Sweden	73	Japan, Norway, Sweden, Finland	79
Norway, Turkey	72	Australia, France, USA	78
Australia, Denmark	71	Canada, Denmark	77
Canada, France, Greece, Italy, Spain, Switzerland, USA	70	Austria, Italy, Spain, Switzerland, West Germany	76
Austria, Belgium, Bulgaria, East Germany, Irish Republic, New Zealand, West Germany, Finland	69	Belgium, East Germany, New Zealand, Taiwan	75
Albania, UK	68	Greece, Czechoslovakia, Hungary, Irish Republic, UK, USSR	74

Countries with the Lowest Expectation of Life

Men	Years	Women	Years
Ethiopia	38	North Yemen	40
Guinea-Bisseau, Gambia, North Yemen	39	Ethiopia	41
Angola, Burundi	40	Afghanistan, Angola, Guinea-Bissau, Burundi, Gambia, Bhutan, Nepal	43
Burkina Faso, Malawi, Mali, Mauritania, Niger, Senegal, Somalia	41	Burkina Faso, Mali, Malawi, Mauritania, Niger, Senegal, Liberia	44
Afghanistan, Guinea, South Yemen, Laos	42	Chad, Guinea, India, South Yemen, Somalia, Gabon	45

The Vocabulary of Age

Age	Word
40–49	quadragenarian
50–59	quinquagenarian
60–69	sexagenarian
70–79	septagenarian
80–89	octogenarian
90–99	nonagenarian
100 or more	centenarian

Growth of Population and Average Life Expectancy

The table below indicates the projected growth in population and the average life expectancy based on 1981 figures. What you must remember is that, although a lot of children will be born, many will die before they reach their teens.

Growth Rate Projected over 5 years

Country	Decline	0%	+5%	+10%	+15%	+20%	Age Men	& Women
Afghanistan				★			42	43
Albania				★			68	71
Algeria				★			56	58
Angola				★			40	43
Argentina			★				65	71
Australia			★				71	78
Austria		★					69	76
Bahamas			★				64	69

Country	Decline	0%	+5%	+10%	+15%	+20%	Age Men & Women	
Bangladesh				★			46	47
Barbados		★					68	72
Belgium	★						69	75
Belize		★					45	49
Benin		★					44	48
Bermuda		★					66	72
Bhutan		★					44	43
Bolivia			★				48	53
Botswana			★				47	50
Brazil			★				58	61
Brunei			★				62	62
Bulgaria			★				67	72
Burkina Faso	★						41	44
Burma					★		56	60
Burundi			★				40	43
Cameroon			★				44	48
Canada		★					70	77
Cape Verde Islands			★				58	62

Country	Decline	0%	+5%	+10%	+15%	+20%	Age Men & Women	
Central African Republic				★			44	48
Chad				★			43	45
Chile			★				61	68
China			★				62	66
Colombia				★			61	64
Congo				★			44	48
Costa Rica				★			66	70
Cuba	★						69	72
Cyprus			★				72	75
Czechoslovakia	★						69	74
Denmark	★						71	77
Dominica				★			58	62
Ecuador					★		60	62
Egypt				★			55	58
El Salvador					★		60	65
Ethiopia					★		38	41
Fiji							70	73
Finland	★						69	79
France	★						70	78

Country	Decline	0%	+5%	+10%	+15%	+20%	Age Men	Women
Gabon							42	45
Gambia							39	43
Germany, East	★						69	75
Germany, West		★					69	76
Ghana					★		47	50
Greece			★				70	74
Grenada							60	66
Guatemala					★		54	56
Guinea				★			42	45
Guinea-Bissau							39	43
Guyana							67	72
Haiti				★			49	52
Honduras					★		49	52
Hong Kong					★		68	72
Hungary	★						69	74
Iceland							74	80
India				★			46	45
Indonesia			★				49	51

Country	Decline	0%	+5%	+10%	+15%	+20%	Age Men	& Women
Iran					★		58	57
Iraq					★		54	57
Ireland		★					69	74
Israel				★			72	76
Italy		★					70	76
Ivory Coast					★		44	48
Jamaica			★				68	73
Japan		★					73	79
Jordan						★	62	66
Kenya						★	54	58
Kiribati							57	59
Korea, North							61	65
Korea, South							63	69
Laos				★			42	45
Liberia							46	44
Libya						★	54	57
Luxemburg		★					63	72
Madagascar				★			44	48
Malawi				★			41	44

Country	Decline	0%	+5%	+10%	+15%	+20%	Age Men	Women
Malaysia					★		67	72
Mali					★		41	44
Mauritania					★		41	44
Mauritius							61	65
Mexico				★			63	67
Mongolia				★			61	65
Morocco					★		54	57
Mozambique				★			44	48
Namibia			★				50	53
Nepal					★		44	43
Netherlands		★					72	79
New Zealand			★				69	75
Nicaragua						★	55	59
Niger					★		41	44
Nigeria					★		46	49
Norway		★					72	79
Oman							46	48
Pakistan					★		52	52
Panama							54	57

Country	Decline	0%	+5%	+10%	+15%	+20%	Age Men	& Women
Papua New Guinea			★				50	50
Paraguay					★		62	65
Peru				★			55	58
Philippines				★			59	62
Poland		★					66	74
Portugal		★					65	73
Romania		★					67	72
Rwanda					★		44	48
St Kitts-Nevis							58	62
Sarawak							51	53
Saudi Arabia					★		47	49
Senegal							41	44
Seychelles							65	71
Sierra Leone				★			44	48
Singapore			★				69	74
Somalia						★	41	45
South Africa					★		59	62
Spain		★					70	76
Sri Lanka			★				62	65

Country	Decline	0%	+5%	+10%	+15%	+20%	Age	Men & Women
Sudan					★		46	48
Surinam							65	70
Sweden		★					73	79
Switzerland		★					70	76
Syria						★	63	75
Taiwan							70	75
Tanzania				★			49	52
Thailand				★			58	63
Togo					★		44	48
Trinidad and Tobago			★				64	68
Tunisia				★			56	58
Turkey				★			57	59
Uganda				★			51	54
UK	★						68	74
USA			★				70	78
USSR			★				64	74
Uruguay			★				66	73
Yemen, North				★			39	40
Yemen, South (PDR)					★		43	45

Country	Decline	0%	+5%	+10%	+15%	+20%	Age Men	& Women
Yugoslavia	★						65	70
Zaire				★			44	48
Zambia				★			47	50
Zimbabwe					★		52	55

Energy

Fossil fuels are the remains of organisms that have a high carbon or hydrogen content, or both. These are coal, gas and oil, but some of the deposits are being used up very quickly and they cannot be replaced, so the search is on to find more. At the same time there is a growing interest in finding alternative sources of power.

Many countries have hydro-electric power stations and many more are being built; others have invested in nuclear power stations. The use of solar and thermal power and that of winds and tides are all being investigated.

The table below shows what deposits of fossil fuels each country has. Some countries have oil but they haven't been included if they produce less than 20 million tonnes a year. The percentage shown under nuclear power shows how much of the country's electricity is supplied by this method. Those countries with nuclear power stations producing less than five per cent have not been included.

Country	Coal	Gas	Oil	Nuclear Power
Afghanistan	★			
Algeria		★	★	
Angola		★	★	
Argentina	★	★		
Australia	★	★	★	

Country	Coal	Gas	Oil	Nuclear Power
Austria	★			
Bahrain			★	
Bangladesh	★	★		
Belgium	★			★ (10%)
Bolivia		★		
Burma	★	★	★	
Cameroon		★		
Canada		★	★	★ (5%)
Chile	★	★	★	
China	★		★	
Colombia			★	
Congo			★	
Czechoslovakia	★			
Ecuador	★		★	
Egypt		★	★	
Finland				★ (20%)
France	★	★		★ (20%)
Gabon		★	★	
Germany, East	★			★ (5%)
Germany, West	★			★ (10%)

Country	Coal	Gas	Oil	Nuclear Power
Hungary	★	★		
India	★		★	
Indonesia			★	
Iran			★	
Iraq			★	
Japan	★			★ (10%)
Korea, North	★			
Korea, South	★			
Kuwait			★	
Libya			★	
Malaysia			★	
Mexico	★	★	★	
Netherlands		★		
New Zealand	★	★		
Nigeria	★	★	★	
Norway		★	★	
Oman		★	★	
Pakistan		★		
Peru			★	
Poland	★			

Country	Coal	Gas	Oil	Nuclear Power
Qatar		★	★	
Romania	★	★		
Saudi Arabia			★	
South Africa	★			
Spain	★			★ (5%)
Swaziland	★			
Sweden				★ (20%)
Switzerland				★ (5%)
Syria			★	
Taiwan	★	★		
Tonga			★	
Trinidad and Tobago	★			
Tunisia			★	
Turkey	★			
United Arab Emirates		★	★	
UK	★	★	★	★ (5%)
USA	★	★	★	★ (5%)
USSR	★	★	★	★ (5%)
Venezuela	★		★	
Vietnam	★			

Country	Coal	Gas	Oil	Nuclear Power
Yugoslavia	★	★		
Zaire			★	
Zambia	★			
Zimbabwe	★			

The Top Ten Importers of Oil

Country	Million tonnes/year
USA	281
Japan	217
France	114
Germany, West	97
Italy	87
Netherlands	50
Spain	49
Brazil	44
UK (but exports almost as much)	43
Belgium	33

The Top Ten Exporters of Oil

Country	Million tonnes/year
Saudi Arabia	462
USSR	122
Iraq	121
Nigeria	97
Libya	82
United Arab Emirates	82
Venezuela	68
Kuwait	64
Indonesia	51
Mexico	41

Organization of Petroleum Exporting Countries (OPEC)

OPEC was formed in 1960 to unify and co-ordinate the petroleum policies of member states, to regulate production and prices, and to protect their own interests. The Conference of Ministers meets at least twice a year to work out policies.

Member States

Algeria	Iraq	Qatar
Ecuador	Kuwait	Saudi Arabia

Member States (Cont.)

Gabon	Libya	United Arab Emirates
Indonesia	Nigeria	Venezuela
Iran		

Some Facts About Energy

○ USA consumes 28.6% of the world's oil
○ the first atomic pile was in action at Stagg Field, University of Chicago, USA, in December 1942
○ the largest oil field in the world is at Ghawar in Saudi Arabia
○ the largest tidal power station is on the estuary of the River Rance in France
○ the largest nuclear power station is near Leningrad, USSR
○ the largest solar furnace is at Bristow, California, USA
○ the largest gas field is in Urengoi, USSR
○ the largest oil platform is the Norwegian *Stratford B* in the North Sea

Mineral Resources

The world's mineral resources are considerable. In some of the countries listed below the minerals have yet to be exploited. This is usually because it will be both difficult and expensive to mine them. There are also valuable reserves in Antarctica, some in the Arctic, and beneath the floor of the oceans.

Symbol	Mineral	Characteristics
(Bx)	bauxite	natural hydrated aluminium oxide; the most important ore in aluminium
Cr	chromium	greyish-white hard metal used in chromium plating and the manufacture of stainless steel
Cu	copper	red malleable metal which can be hammered or pressed into shape without breaking; unaffected by water or steam and the best conductor of electricity; also used in alloys

Symbol	Mineral	Characteristics
Fe	iron	silvery-white malleable magnetic metal obtained by smelting in a blast furnace
Pb	lead	bluish white soft metal; resistant to corrosion; widely used in alloys and as a shield against X-rays and radiation
Mn	manganese	whitish hard, brittle element found in many ores; used in many alloys and steels
Ni	nickel	silvery-white soft malleable metal; used for nickel plating and in many alloys
Sn	tin	silvery-white soft malleable metal unaffected by air or water at normal temperatures; used for tin plating and in many alloys
Zn	zinc	bluish-white hard metal; used in alloys such as bronze, brass and nickel silver
U	uranium	radioactive element found in pitchblende and other ores; used in nuclear reactors and nuclear weapons

Note: numbers indicate countries with the greatest amount of each mineral.

Country	(Bx)	Cr	Cu	Fe	Pb	Mn	Ni	Sn	Zn	U
Afghanistan			★	★	★					
Albania		★4								
Algeria		★	★	★					★	
Angola				★						
Argentina			★							
Australia	★1		★	★3	★3	★7	★3		★5	★
Bolivia	★		★		★			★4	★	
Botswana							★			
Brazil	★5			★2		★3		★		

178

Country	(Bx)	Cr	Cu	Fe	Pb	Mn	Ni	Sn	Zn	U
Bulgaria			★	★		★			★	
Burkina Faso	★		★			★	★2			
Burma					★			★	★	
Burundi								★		
Cameroon	★							★		
Canada		★5	★3	★6	★4		★1		★1	★2
Central African Republic										★
Chile		★3	★1	★						
China				★5		★4		★5		
Colombia			★		★	★				
Comoros			★							
Congo					★			★	★	
Cuba		★	★	★		★8	★			
Czecholsovakia				★						★
Dominica	★		★	★						
Gabon				★		★5				
Germany, West				★						
Ghana	★					★				
Gibraltar				★						

Country	(Bx)	Cr	Cu	Fe	Pb	Mn	Ni	Sn	Zn	U
Greece	★			★			★			
Guatemala							★			
Guinea	★4			★						★
Guinea-Bissau	★			★						
Guyana	★			★						
Haiti	★		★							
Honduras					★				★	
Hungary	★									
India				★7			★5			
Indonesia								★3		
Irish Republic					★				★	
Jamaica	★3									
Japan		★		★	★				★	
Korea, North			★	★	★					
Laos								★		
Liberia				★						
Luxemburg				★						
Malaysia								★		
Mauritania			★	★						
Mexico	★			★	★				★	

Country	(Bx)	Cr	Cu	Fe	Pb	Mn	Ni	Sn	Zn	U
Morocco			★	★	★				★	
Namibia										★5
New Caledonia							★			
New Hebrides						★				
Nicaragua			★						★	
Niger										★4
Nigeria				★						
Niue										★
Norway			★	★						
Oman			★							
Peru			★	★	★5				★4	
Philippines		★	★	★			★6			
Poland			★	★.						
Portugal				★						
Rwanda							★			
Sierra Leone	★			★						
Solomon Islands	★									
South Africa		★1	★	★		★2				★3
Spain			★	★	★	★			★	
Sudan			★	★		★				

Country	(Bx)	Cr	Cu	Fe	Pb	Mn	Ni	Sn	Zn	U
Surinam	★			★						
Swaziland								★		
Sweden			★	★	★				★	
Taiwan			★							
Thailand								★		
Turkey			★	★						
Uganda			★							
UK				★						
USA	★2		★	★4	★1				★5	★1
USSR	★7	★2	★2	★1	★2	★1	★	★2	★2	
Venezuela	★			★	★					
Vietnam		★		★				★		
Yugoslavia	★	★	★	★						
Zaire			★5						★	
Zambia			★4						★	
Zimbabwe	★6	★	★				★			

Some Facts about Mines

○ The earliest mine discovered is thought to have been first worked in about 40,000 BC. It is close to Hhohho in Swaziland.
○ The largest open-cast copper mine is Bingham Canyon close to Salt Lake City, Utah, USA. About 1,200 million m^3 of material has been excavated since it opened in 1904.

- The largest uranium mine is the Rio Tinto open-cast pit in Rössing in Namibia.
- The largest lead mine is Viburnum Trend in Missouri, USA.

Precious Metals and Diamonds

Gold, silver and diamonds as well as other precious stones have been prized since the earliest times, and the desire to possess them has led to wars and to the opening up of new territories, as happened in the Yukon, in the USA and in Australia.

All the countries listed below are currently producing precious metals and diamonds. Countries with a very low level of production have not been included

Country	Gold	Silver	Platinum	Diamonds	Industrial Diamonds
Afghanistan	★				
Angola				★	
Argentina	★	★			
Australia	★	★			
Bolivia	★				
Botswana				★	★
Brazil	★			★	
Burma		★			
Burkina Faso	★				
Burundi	★			★	
Cameroon	★				
Canada	★	★	★3		

Country	Gold	Silver	Platinum	Diamonds	Industrial Diamonds
Central African Republic				★	
Colombia	★	★	★	★	
Fiji	★				
Ghana	★			★	
Guinea	★			★	
Guyana	★				
Honduras	★	★			
Irish Republic	★	★			
Kenya	★				
Lesotho				★	
Liberia				★	
Mexico	★	★1			
Namibia				★3	
Nicaragua	★				
Peru		★2			
Philippines	★				
Poland		★			
Sierra Leone				★	
South Africa	★1		★2	★1	★3

Country	Gold	Silver	Platinum	Diamonds	Industrial Diamonds
Sudan	★				
Swaziland	★				
Tanzania				★	
USA	★	★	★		
USSR	★2	★3	★1	★2	★1
Upper Volta	★				
Venezuala	★			★	
Vietnam	★				
Zaire				★	★2
Zambia		★			

Some Facts about Precious Metals and Diamonds

○ The largest diamond ever found was the Cullinan which weighed 3,106 metric carats (1.25 lb). From it was cut the Star of Africa, now in the Royal Sceptre. This weighed over 530 metric carats.

○ The largest nugget of gold found was part of a slab of slate from the Beyers and Holtermann Star of Hope mine in Hill End, New South Wales, Australia. The 285.7 kg piece of slate held gold weighing 99.8 kg.

○ The deepest gold mine in the world (3,777 m) is in Carletonville, South Africa.

○ The world's largest gold mine, covering 4,900 ha., is in Boksburgh in the Transvaal, South Africa.

○ The USA has the greatest gold reserves in the world.

Drink

Everyone has to drink. A person takes in an average of 2.6 litres of fluids a day, and absorbs more through food. Men only had water to drink at first, but as they domesticated animals, so milk was available. It wasn't long before grapes were cultivated and wine made, and beer was brewed practically everywhere. Later, in other parts of the world, tea, coffee and cacao (cocoa) were grown and turned into beverages.

Country	Coffee	Tea	Cocoa	Wine
Angola	★			
Argentina				★
Austria				★
Australia				★
Bangladesh		★		
Benin	★			
Bolivia	★		★	
Brazil	★			★
Bulgaria				★
Burundi	★			
Cameroon	★		★	
Central African Republic	★			
Chile				★
China		★		★
Comoros	★		★	

Country	Coffee	Tea	Cocoa	Wine
Congo	★		★	
Costa Rica	★			
Cyprus				★
Czechoslovakia				★
Dominica	★		★	
Ecuador	★			★
Egypt				★
El Salvador	★		★	
Equatorial Guinea	★		★	
Ethiopia	★			
France				★
Germany, East				★
Germany, West				★
Ghana		★		
Greece				★
Guatemala	★			
Guinea	★			
Haiti	★			
Honduras	★			
Hungary				★

Country	Coffee	Tea	Cocoa	Wine
India		★		
Indonesia	★			
Israel				★
Italy				★
Ivory Coast	★		★	
Jamaica	★		★	
Japan				★
Kenya	★			
Laos	★			
Lebanon				★
Liberia	★		★	
Madagascar	★			
Malta				★
Mexico	★			
Morocco				★
Mozambique		★		
Nicaragua	★			
Peru				★
Portugal				★
Réunion		★		

Country	Coffee	Tea	Cocoa	Wine
Romania				★
Rwanda	★		★	
São Tomé and Principe			★	
Sierra Leone	★	★	★	
Solomon Islands	★		★	
South Africa				★
Spain				★
Sri Lanka		★		
Switzerland				★
Tanzania	★			
Togo	★		★	
Trinidad and Tobago	★		★	
Tunisia				★
Turkey				★
Uganda	★	★		
UK				★
USA				★
USSR		★		★
Uruguay				★
Venezuela	★		★	

Country	Coffee	Tea	Cocoa	Wine
Vietnam		★		
Yemen, North	★			
Yugoslavia				★

Some Facts about Drinks and Drinkers

○ The greatest consumers of coffee are the Finns.
○ The greatest consumers of tea are the Irish.
○ The greatest consumers of wine are the French.
○ The greatest consumers of beer are the West Germans.
○ More than seventy-five per cent of the world's wine is made in Europe.
○ There were probably vineyards in Egypt and Phoenicia as early as 6,000 BC.

The Staples of Life

Cereals, including rice, are eaten by people all over the world, but few countries are able to grow enough to feed their populations.

The table below shows the main exporting countries. A country exporting wheat, for instance, might have to import rice, but if it exports more than it imports, it has been included.

Exporters of Cereals

Argentina	France	South Africa
Austria	Guyana	Sweden
Australia	Hungary	Thailand
Burma	New Zealand	Turkey
Canada	Pakistan	USA
Denmark		

Plenty and Hunger

If you consider the number of calories available for each person, some countries have a great deal more and others a great deal less than the average requirement to lead a healthy life. The countries are listed in alphabetical order.

Best Fed Countries in the World

* Argentina
Australia
* Austria
* Belgium
* Bulgaria
* Canada
Cuba
Cyprus
* Czechoslovakia
* Denmark
Finland
* France
Gabon
* Germany, East
* Germany, West
* Hungary
* Irish Republic
Israel
* Italy
Ivory Coast
Jamaica
Japan
* Korea, South
Lebanon
* Libya
Malta
Mexico
New Guinea
* New Zealand
Norway
Papua New Guinea
Philippines

Worst Fed Countries in the World

† Afghanistan
Angola
† Bangladesh
Bolivia
Botswana
Burkina Faso
Burundi
Central African Republic
Colombia
Djibouti
Dominica
Ecuador
El Salvador
† Ethiopia
Gambia
Guatemala
† Guinea
India
† Kampuchea
Kenya
† Laos
Malawi
† Mali
Mauritania
Morocco
Mozambique
Nepal
Niger
Rwanda
Senegal
Sierra Leone
Somalia

Best Fed Countries in the World

* Poland
* Portugal
* Romania
  South Africa
* Spain
  Sweden
  Syria
  Tunisia
* UK
* USA
* USSR
* Yugoslavia

* The very best fed countries (consume 25% *more* calories than needed).

Worst Fed Countries in the World

† Sudan
  Togo
† Uganda
  Vietnam
  Yemen, North
† Yemen, South
  Zaire
† Zimbabwe

† The very worst fed countries (consume at least 15% *fewer* calories than needed).

Famines

Famines are not always caused by lack of rain or a sudden change in climate. Sometimes they are caused by man. War often leads to starvation since people are unable, or too afraid, to work on the land.

Famines Since 1950

Year	Countries Affected	Continent
1950	India	Southern Asia
	Pakistan	
1951	India	Southern Asia
	Pakistan	
1952	India	Southern Asia
	Pakistan	
1953	India	Southern Asia
	Pakistan	
1954	Haiti	Caribbean
	India	Southern Asia
	Pakistan	
	Vietnam	South East Asia
1956	Pakistan	Southern Asia

Year	Countries Affected	Continent
1960	Chile	South America
	Congo	Africa
	Mauritania	Africa
	Morocco	Africa, North
	Pakistan	Southern Asia
1961	Congo	Africa
	Vietnam	South East Asia
1963	Algeria	Africa, North
1964	Vietnam	South East Asia
1965	India	Southern Asia
1966	India	Southern Asia
1967	India	Southern Asia
	Nigeria	Africa
	Colombia	South America
1968	Nigeria	Africa
	Vietnam	South East Asia
1969	Nigeria	Africa
1970	Nigeria	Africa
	Bangladesh	Southern Asia
	Kampuchea	South East Asia
	Peru	South America
1971	Angola	Africa
	Burkina Faso	
	Chad	
	Ghana	
	Mozambique	
	Niger	
	Togo	
	Pakistan	Southern Asia
	Bangladesh	
1972	Angola	Africa
	Chad	
	Ghana	
	Mauritania	
	Mozambique	
	Niger	
	Togo	
	Pakistan	Southern Asia
	Bangladesh	
	Nicaragua	Central America
	Philippines	South East Asia

Year	Countries Affected	Continent
1973	Chad	Africa
	Ethiopia	
	Ghana	
	Mozambique	
	Mauritania	
	Niger	
	Sudan	
	Togo	
	Bangladesh	Southern Asia
	Pakistan	
1974	Angola	Africa
	Chad	
	Central African Republic	
	Ethiopia	
	Gambia	
	Mozambique	
	Niger	
	Nigeria	
	Lesotho	
	Somalia	
	Togo	
	Mauritania	
	Bangladesh	Southern Asia
1975	Ethiopia	Africa
	Somalia	
	Bangladesh	Southern Asia
	Kampuchea	South East Asia
	Vietnam	
	Haiti	Caribbean
1976	Ethiopia	Africa
	Indonesia	South East Asia
	Kampuchea	
	Haiti	Caribbean
1977	Burkina Faso	Africa
	Ethiopia	
	Togo	
	Indonesia	South East Asia
1978	Ethiopia	Africa
	Indonesia	South East Asia
1978	Kampuchea	South East Asia

Year	Countries Affected	Continent
1979	Zambia	Africa
	Kampuchea	South East Asia
1980	Ethiopia	Africa
	Uganda	
1981	Brazil	South America
1982	Brazil	South America
1983	Angola	Africa
	Chad	
	Djibouti	
	Ethiopia	
	Lesotho	
	Mauritania	
	Mozambique	
	Swaziland	
	Tanzania	
	Togo	
	Zambia	
1984	Ethiopia	Africa
1985	Ethiopia	Africa
	Sudan	

7 WAR

From City-State to Empire

City-states were founded, prospered, developed into empires, and fell. Some lasted longer than others. The Egyptians, whose history went back to before 5,000 BC and whose empire expanded dramatically and contracted equally remarkably, were not fully conquered until 322 BC. The Persians, who defeated the Medes, were in their turn defeated by the Greeks, and the Greeks were then conquered by the Romans.

The Roman Republic and the Roman Empire

Year BC	Event
753	foundation of Rome (traditional)
510	foundation of Roman Republic
290	conquest of central Italy
264–41	first Punic War against Carthage
218–1	second Punic War against Carthage
215–146	war with Greece
206	control of Spain
168	defeat of Macedonia
149–6	third Punic War against Carthage; Carthage destroyed
146	Corinth sacked
146	province of North Africa established
64	conquest of Syria
49	conquest of Gaul
27	end of Roman Republic; beginning of Roman Empire

Year AD	Event
43	invasion of Britain by Claudius
44	Morocco annexed
70	Temple of Jerusalem destroyed
116	conquest of Mesopotamia
132	Jewish rebellion suppressed; Jews dispersed
238	start of struggle against the Goths
330	Rome abandoned; Constantinople becomes the capital of the Roman Empire

Year AD	Event
370	Huns appear in Europe
378	defeat of Romans at the battle of Adrianople by mixed tribes of Goths, Huns and others
406	Vandals invade Gaul
407	Vandals invade Spain
410	Vandals invade Italy and sack Rome

Note: although the western empire collapsed, Byzantium, the eastern empire, managed to exist until 1453 when its capital, Constantinople, was captured by the Turks.

The Spread of Islam

What was remarkable about the domination of Muslims throughout Arabia, the Gulf, Egypt, North Africa, Spain and into Pakistan and the USSR, was the speed at which it was accomplished.

Year AD	Event
636	defeat of Romans at the battle of Yarmuk
636	conquest of Syria
638	conquest of Iraq
642	conquest of Egypt; expansion along the North African coast
642–3	conquest of Persia
664	fall of Kabul
673	unsuccessful attack on Constantinople
711	Spain invaded
712	crossing of the Indus; Sind in Pakistan occupied; penetration to Samarkand
717	unsuccessful seige of Constantinople
732	defeat at the battle of Poitiers and withdrawal from France to Spain
753	victory over the Chinese at the battle of the River Talus
762	Baghdad founded as the new capital of the Abbasid dynasty

Note: the further expansion of Islam is largely the story of the Seljuk Turks, the Ottoman Turks, and missionary zeal of the Muslim traders as they expanded into Africa and South East Asia.

Battles

Battles are no longer set pieces where armies confront each other: one advancing and the other resisting. Nor are they over quickly these days. The battle of Midway Island, a naval engagement, was one in which the sailors in the American and Japanese ships didn't even see each other. The attacks were carried out by naval aircraft.

Some of the battles listed below really did change the course of history, but many were just one of a series in long-lasting wars.

Year BC	Battle	Event
612	Nineveh	Assyrian capital of Nineveh captured and destroyed by the Medes; Assyrian power in the Middle East ended
593	Babylon	King Cyrus the Great of Persia captured Babylon
490	Marathon	Persian attack on Athens defeated by the Greeks
324–9	series of battles	Alexander the Great of Macedon conquered Asia Minor, Egypt (332), Persia (330) and reached India (329)
216	Cannae	Hannibal of Carthage defeated the Romans
146	Carthage	Carthage destroyed by Romans
146	Corinth	Corinth sacked by Romans; Rome dominant in the Mediterranean
31	Actium	naval battle in which Octavius (later Emperor Augustus) defeated Anthony and Cleopatra

Year AD		
43	Brentwood	Emperor Claudius of Rome defeated the British
61	Verulamium (St Albans)	Queen Boadicea defeated by Romans
410	Rome	Rome sacked by Visigoths

Year AD	Battle	Event
732	Tours	Frankish army defeated massed cavalry thus stemming the advance of the Moors into Europe from Spain
878	Ethandune	King Alfred the Great defeated the Danes
1066	Hastings	William the Conqueror of Normandy defeated the Saxon King Harold and was crowned King of England
1071	Manzikert	Seljuk Turks defeated the army of Byzantium and established power over Asia Minor
1314	Bannockburn	Edward II defeated by Scottish led by Robert Bruce
1346	Crécy	large French army commanded by King Philip defeated by small British force under Edward III (Hundred Years' War)
1410	Tannenburg	Teutonic knights advance into Europe stemmed by Poles and Lithuanians
1415	Agincourt	Henry V's small army defeated French led by Louis, Duke of Orleans (Hundred Years' War)
1429	Patay	Joan of Arc led the French to victory against the English (Hundred Years' War)
1453	Constantinople	Ottoman Turks captured Byzantine capital
1461	Towton	Yorkists defeated Lancastrians; 28,000 killed (Wars of the Roses)
1485	Bosworth	Richard III defeated by Henry Tudor who was crowned as Henry VII
1512	Ravenna	Gaston de Foix of France defeated large Spanish army

Year AD	Battle	Event
1526	Mohacs	Ottoman Turks defeated Hungarians and overran the whole country
1571	Lepanto	sea-battle ended Turkish naval power in the Mediterranean
1578	Al Kasr al Kebir	Moroccans ended Portuguese domination of north-west Africa
1588	Armada	Spanish Armada defeated by British
1614	Surat	British East India Company ships defeated Portuguese
1645	Naseby	Roundheads, led by Cromwell and Fairfax, defeated Royalists under Prince Rupert of the Rhine; last battle of the English Civil War; King Charles I subsequently executed
1672	Sole Bay	naval battle in which the Dutch beat the British
1690	Boyne	William of Orange (William III) defeated James II
1704	Blenheim	Duke of Marlborough defeated the combined French and Bavarian armies; over 50,000 casualties (War of Spanish Succession)
1757	Plassey	Robert Clive defeated Surajah Dowlah in India although outnumbered by seventeen to one
1759	Quebec	General Wolfe defeated the French in Canada (Seven Years' War)
1775	Bunker Hill	General Howe's forces defeated American irregulars, but glory gained by the Americans (War of American Independence)
1781	Yorktown	British surrendered to American and French forces; Americans gained their independence
1798	Nile	British fleet commanded by Lord Nelson defeated the French navy in Aboukir Bay (Napoleonic Wars)

Year AD	Battle	Event
1800	Marengo	Napoleon defeated Austrian army (Napoleonic Wars)
1805	Trafalgar	British defeated the combined French and Spanish navies, but Lord Nelson was killed
1805	Austerlitz	French led by Napoleon defeated a combined Russian and Austrian army; over 150,000 men fought in the battle
1811	Tippencanoe	Americans defeated the confederency of Indian tribes
1812	Borodino	240,000 French and Russian troops fought; the Russians withdrew and Napoleon reached Moscow but was forced to retreat (Napoleonic Wars)
1813	Vittoria	Wellesley (Duke of Wellington) defeated the French and crossed the Pyrénées
1815	Waterloo	British under Wellington defeated Napoleon with the aid of the Prussians under Blücher
1827	Navarino	naval battle during the Greek War of Independence in which British, French and Russian ships destroyed the combined Turkish and Egyptian navies
1836 (March)	Alamo	Alamo was a defeat for the Texans, 180 volunteers versus several thousand Mexicans. All defenders killed; Davy Crockett among the last to die.
1836 (April)	San Janito	American settlers in Texas defeated the Mexican army; Texas subsequently annexed to the USA
1854	Balaklava	Russians failed to seize the British base, but confusion led to the brave but pointless Charge of the Light Brigade (Crimean War)

Year AD	Battle	Event
1863	Gettysburg	General Meade defeated the Confederates under General Lee; this was a turning point in the American Civil War
1866	Sadowa	Prussians defeated Austrians and established dominance of German states
1876	Little Big Horn	small force led by General Custer wiped out by Sioux Indians
1879	Ulundi	Zulu success in battle against the British in Africa halted when Sir Garnet Wolsely defeated Cetewayo
1914	Tannenberg	the Russian advance into Germany halted; 100,000 taken prisoner
1916	Somme	twenty weeks of fighting by British, French and Commonwealth troops against the Germans; the allies gained about ten miles of territory and lost 100,000 men
1917	Caporetto	Austrians defeated the Italians; nearly 300,000 taken prisoner
1939	Plate	German battleship *Graf Spee* badly damaged by the British navy and subsequently scuttled
1940	Britain	long conflict between the RAF and the German Luftwaffe from 10 June until late October; 1,733 German and 915 British aircraft lost; planned invasion of Britain was no longer possible
1941	Pearl Harbor	surprise Japanese attack on US air base in Hawaii; brought USA into the Second World War
1942	Midway	USA won a decisive naval battle against the Japanese; Japanese expansion into the central Pacific brought to an end

Year AD	Battle	Event
1942	El Alamein	fifteen day battle in the desert fought by British and allied troops resulted in the subsequent withdrawal of German and Italian troops from North Africa
1942–3	Stalingrad	Russian forces fiercely resisted Germans, under General von Paulus, with street to street fighting; Germans then besieged by a Russian relief force under General Zhukov and forced to surrender; 90,000 prisoners
1944	Cassino	constant attacks by British and allied forces finally successful, resulting in the fall of Rome
1944	Ardennes	final effort made by German forces to halt the allied advance into Germany failed
1952	Dien Bien Phu	French defeated by the Viet Minh; French withdrew from North Vietnam

---

Wars During the Last Two Hundred Years

Men have constantly been engaged in conflict. Listed below are some of the wars that have taken place during the last two hundred years. The many border conflicts have not been included.

War	Dates	Main Combatants
War of the Grand Alliance	1689–97	Britain, Holland, Austria v France
Great Northern War	1700–21	Russia v Sweden
Turkish-Austrian War	1737–9	Turkey v Austria
Seven Years' War	1756–63	Britain v France
Russo-Turkish War	1768–74	Russia v Turkey

War	Dates	Main Combatants
War of American Independence	1775–83	Britain v America, France, Spain
Russo-Turkish War	1787–92	Russia v Turkey
Napoleonic Wars		
1st Coalition	1792–7	(Britain engaged in all these wars against France in various coalitions involving Austria, Prussia, Russia, Portugal, Spain and others)
2nd Coalition	1798–1801	
3rd Coalition	1805–7	
Peninsular War	1809–14	
Anglo-American War	1812–14	
4th Coalition	1813–14	
Russo-Turkish War	1806–12	Russia v Turkey
Indian (American) War	1811	Americans v Indians
Greek War of Independence	1821–30	Greece v Turkey
Ashanti War	1824–7	Britain v Ashanti
Burma War	1824–6	Britain v Burma
Indian (American) War	1816–18	Americans v Indians
Indian (American) War	1835–42	Americans v Indians
Afghan War	1838–42	Britain v Afghans
Opium War	1839–42	Britain v China
First Maori War	1843	Britain v Maoris
Mexican War	1846–8	Mexico v America
Crimean War	1853–6	Russia v France, Turkey and Britain
Austro-Piedmontese French War	1859	Austria v Piedmont, France
Second Maori War	1860–70	Britain v Maoris
American Civil War	1861–5	America
Spanish-Cuban War	1869–78	Spain v Cuba
Seven Weeks' War	1866	Austria v Prussia
Carlist War	1870–6	Spain
Franco-Prussian War	1870–1	France v Prussia
Ashanti War	1873–4	Britain v Ashanti
Russo-Turkish War	1877–8	Russia v Turkey

War	Dates	Main Combatants
Afghan War	1878–9	Britain v Afghans
Zulu War	1879	Britain v Zulus
Boer War	1881	Britain v Boers
Burma War	1885–6	Britain v Burma
Sino-Japanese War	1894–5	China v Japan
Spanish-American War	1898	USA v Spain
Boer War	1899–1902	Britain v Boers
Russo-Japanese War	1904–5	Russia v Japan
Italian-Turkish War	1911–12	Italy v Turkey
Balkan Wars	1912–13	Turkey v Balkan States; Balkan States v Greece
First World War	1914–18	Germany, Austro-Hungary, Turkey v France, USSR, Britain, Commonwealth and many other states including Japan, USA, Italy
Russo-Lithuanian War	1919–20	Russia v Lithuania
Polish-Russian War	1919–21	Russia v Poland
Abyssinian War	1935–6	Italy v Abyssinia
Spanish Civil War	1936–9	Spain
Sino-Japanese War	1937–45	China v Japan
Russo-Finnish War	1939–40	Russia v Finland
Second World War	1939–45	Germany, Italy and later Japan v France, Britain, Commonwealth, Russia and later USA with other forces
Chinese Civil War	1945–8	China
Franco-Vietnamese War	1946–54	France v Vietnam
Egypt-Israeli War	1948	Egypt v Israel
Korean War	1950–3	North Korea, Chinese 'volunteers' v South Koreans and UN contingents

War	Dates	Main Combatants
Suez	1956	France, Israel, Britain v Egypt, Syria
Vietnamese War	1959–75	civil war, with US involvement
Six Day War	1967	Egypt, Syria, Jordan v Israel
Iran-Iraq War	1980 to present	Iran v Iraq
Israeli-Lebanese War	1982–5	Israel v Lebanese, Palestinians
Falklands War	1982	Britain v Argentina

Revolutions

A revolution is the overthrowing of a government or an oppressive regime, but often today it also refers to a military *coup d'état*. The two important years of revolution in Europe, 1830 and 1848, often resulted in popular uprisings some of which were subsequently put down. Nevertheless, they were not failures since they did accelerate social and political changes.

In the list below, revolutions that did not succeed, such as the rising in Hungry in 1956, have not been included, nor have all military *coups d'état*. South America has not been fully covered since the rebellions against Spain and Portugal were complex and led to conflicts between the newly liberated states.

Country	Date
Abyssinia	1974
Aden	1965–7
Afghanistan	1973, 1978, 1979
Albania	1925
Algeria	1954–62
Angola	1975
Argentina	1810–16, 1930, 1945
Belgium	1830
Benin	1963
Brazil	1889
Brunswick	1830
Bulgaria	1875
Chile	1818-21, 1973

Country	Date
China	1911, 1945–9
Colombia	1819
Congo	1960
Corsica	1793
Cuba	1958
Cyprus	1954–9
Denmark	1848–9
Ecuador	1822
Egypt	1919–22, 1952
Finland	1905
France	1789–94, 1830, 1848
Ghana	1979, 1981
Greece	1862, 1967, 1974
Grenada	1979
Guatemala	1944
Haiti	1791, 1986
Indonesia	1945
Iran	1925, 1979
Iraq	1958, 1963
Italy	1848
Lesotho	1985
Libya	1969
Mexico	1867, 1910
Morocco	1953–5
Nigeria	1983, 1985
Pakistan	1971–2
Palestine	1946–7
Panama	1903
Paraguay	1811
Peru	1821–4
Philippines	1899–1902, 1986
Portugal	1910, 1974
Saudi Arabia	1902
Saxony	1830
Southern Rhodesia (Zimbabwe)	1965
Sudan	1882–6
Sweden	1527
Syria	1925–7, 1945

Year AD

Tunisia	1955–6
Turkey	1908, 1919
Uganda	1985
UK	1642–9
USA	1776–1787
USSR	1905, 1917
Uruguay	1825
Venezuela	1821
Yemen, North	1962
Yemen, South	1986

The Development of Weapons

(see also Science and Mathematics: The Development of Transport)

The first weapons were whatever was to hand – lumps of stone and hunks of wood. Man soon learned that if he was going to fight, he had to protect himself, so it wasn't long before he made shields of skin stretched over wooden frames. Within a short time he had made clumsy axes, and before long, he had produced quite a wide range of weapons.

Year BC	Weapon
200,000	wooden spears in use
3,500	clubs, axes and spears used in Ur; wooden carts protected by leather
1,680	chariots and bronze scale-armour used by Hyskos against the Egyptians
1,000	bows, chariots and cavalry used by Assyrians; missiles projected by slings
600	fighting towers used by Assyrians when assaulting Jerusalem

Year AD	
300	chain mail manufactured
1346	primitive cannon used at the battle of Crécy; iron pots, containing gunpowder, hurled stones and iron balls at the enemy

1420	wooden carts with portholes, through which cannon are fired; used by Hussites against Bohemians
1453	sulphur fumes used as a gas by the Turks against the defenders of Constantinople
c.1500	matchlock pistols in use
1615	first reliable flintlock gun produced, but others invented earlier
1640	bayonets in use
1678	ring bayonets in use; soldier able to keep bayonet in position whilst firing
1718	James Puckle invents first practical machine gun, but not adopted
1784	Henry Shrapnel invents an exploding shell
1794	balloons used by French for observation
1805	rockets used by the British in the naval bombardment of Boulogne, but a type of rocket also used against *them* in India c. 1780
1827	breech-loading rifle invented by Von Dreyse
1835	Samuel Colt invents repeating pistol with revolving chamber
1849	Austrians attempt aerial bombardment of Venice with bombs carried over walls by balloons, but results not very successful
1851	breech-loading cannon manufactured by Krupps
1861	Americans use railways to rush troops to the front during the American Civil War
1862	hydraulic system used with cannon so that the recoil shock is absorbed, and the guncarriage remains stationary
1863	Gatling machine gun produced in USA
1885	Hiram Maxim produces first fully automatic machine gun
1906	Dreadnought, the first heavy-armoured battleship, launched by Britain
1908	specification for an aircraft to be used in wartime issued by US Navy Department
1911	aircraft used by Italians for observation in war against Turkey
1912	use of an armoured car by Italians in the same war
1914	French use flame warfare

Year AD

1914	Germans use tear gas against the French
1915	Germans use chlorine gas against the French and Canadians
1915	British build the tank; first used in 1916
1917	Germans use liquid mustard gas
1917	Italians produce the first sub-machine gun
1922	Browning lightweight automatic rifle produced by USA
1936	first mass airlift of troops; 10,000 transported from Morocco to Spain
1938	Japanese use blister gas against the Chinese
1942	Russians produce Katyushas, the first production-type rocket projectors mounted on lorries
1945	atomic bomb dropped on Hiroshima on 6 August

Defence

Expenditure on Defence

It is not easy to find out exactly how much each country spends on defence. Sometimes what they spend, and what they say they spend, are quite different, and it is not always easy to get up-to-date figures.

(GNP means Gross National Product. Very roughly, this is the national income.)

Highest Spenders of GNP	Lowest Spenders of GNP
Albania (4%–10%)	Austria (under 2%)
Brunei (4%–10%)	Bangladesh (under 2%)
Chad (4%–10%)	Barbados (under 2%)
Chile (4%–10%)	Benin (under 2%)
China (4%–10%)	Brazil (under 2%)
Egypt (4%–10%)	Cameroon (under 2%)
Ethiopia (4%–10%)	Colombia (under 2%)
Greece (4%–10%)	Costa Rica (under 1%)
Iran (10%)	Cyprus (under 2%)
Iraq (10%)	Dominica (under 2%)
Israel (10%)	Finland (under 2%)
Jordan (10%)	Ghana (under 1%)
Kuwait (4%–10%)	Guatemala (under 2%)
Laos (10%)	Haiti (under 2%)

Highest Spenders of GNP

Mauritania (10%)
Morocco (4%–10%)
Pakistan (4%–10%)
Peru (4%–10%)
Qatar (4%–10%)
Saudi Arabia (10%)
Singapore (4%–10%)
South Africa (4%–10%)
Sudan (4%–10%)
Syria (10%)
Taiwan (4%–10%)
Turkey (4%–10%)
United Arab Emirates (4%–10%)
UK (4%–10%)
USA (4%–10%)
USSR (10%)
Vietnam (10%)
Yemen, North (4%–10%)
Yemen, South (4%–10%)
Yugoslavia (4%–10%)
Zambia (4%–10%)
Zimbabwe (4%–10%)

Lowest Spenders of GNP

Irish Republic (under 2%)
Jamaica (under 1%)
Japan (under 1%)
Liberia (under 2%)
Luxemburg (under 1%)
Mexico (under 1%)
Nepal (under 1%)
New Zealand (under 2%)
Panama (under 1%)
Papua New Guinea (under 2%)
Paraguay (under 2%)
Romania (under 2%)
Rwanda (under 2%)
Sierra Leone (under 1%)
Spain (under 2%)
Sri Lanka (under 2%)
Swaziland (under 1%)
Switzerland (under 1%)
Trinidad and Tobago (under 1%)
Venezuela (under 2%)

The Manufacture of Arms

A surprising number of countries manufacture armaments, but comparatively few export them. Many of those listed under 'aerospace' either put aircraft together from parts supplied by other countries or build them in conjunction with other countries. Countries capable of building ships very often build nothing larger than coastal craft. Minor arms makers have not been included.

Country	Guns/ Munitions	Military Vehicles	Ships	Aerospace
Algeria	★			
Argentina	★	★	★	★

Country	Guns/Munitions	Military Vehicles	Ships	Aerospace
Australia	★		★	★
Bangladesh			★	
Belgium	★	★	★	★
Brazil	★	★	★	★
Bulgaria	★			
Burma	★		★	
Canada	★	★	★	★
Chile	★			★
China	★	★	★	★
Colombia	★		★	★
Congo	★			
Czechoslovakia	★	★		★
Dominican Republic			★	
Egypt	★	★	★	★
Equatorial Guinea	★			
Ethiopia	★			
Finland	★	★	★	★
France	★	★	★	★
Gabon			★	
Germany, East	★	★	★	

Country	Guns/ Munitions	Military Vehicles	Ships	Aerospace
Germany, West	★	★	★	★
Ghana	★			
Greece	★	★	★	★
Hungary	★	★		
India	★	★	★	★
Indonesia	★		★	★
Iran	★			
Israel	★	★	★	★
Italy	★	★	★	★
Ivory Coast				★
Japan	★	★	★	★
Korea, North	★	★	★	★
Korea, South	★	★	★	★
Kuwait	★			
Libya				★
Madagascar		★		
Malaysia	★		★	
Mexico	★		★	★
Morocco	★			
Netherlands	★	★	★	★

Country	Guns/ Munitions	Military Vehicles	Ships	Aerospace
New Zealand	★		★	★
Nigeria	★		★	★
Norway	★	★	★	★
Pakistan	★		★	★
Papua New Guinea				★
Paraguay				★
Peru	★		★	★
Philippines	★		★	★
Poland	★	★	★	★
Portugal	★	★	★	★
Romania	★	★	★	★
Saudi Arabia	★			
Singapore	★		★	
South Africa	★	★	★	★
Spain	★	★	★	★
Sri Lanka			★	
Sudan	★			
Sweden	★	★	★	★
Syria	★			
Taiwan	★		★	★

Country	Guns/ Munitions	Military Vehicles	Ships	Aerospace
Thailand			★	★
Turkey	★	★	★	★
United Arab Emirates	★			
UK	★	★	★	★
USA	★	★	★	★
USSR	★	★	★	★
Venezuela			★	
Yugoslavia	★	★	★	★

Main Exporters of Arms	Main Importers of Arms (by region)
1 USSR	1 Middle East
2 USA	2 Africa
3 France	3 Far East
4 Italy	4 Central and South America
5 UK	5 Southern Asia
6 Germany, West	

Armed Forces: The Largest in the World

Country	Size	Compulsory Service	Population in Services %
China	4,000,000		0.4
USSR	3,705,000	★	1.4
Indonesia	2,690,000	★	1.8
Iran	2,350,000	★	6.2
USA	2,116,000		0.9
India	1,104,000		0.2
Vietnam	1,029,000	★	1.9

Country	Size	Compulsory Service	Population in Services %
Korea, North	784,000	★	4.4
Korea, South	601,000	★	1.6
Sudan	580,000	★	3.1

Armed Forces in Some Other Countries

Country	Size	Compulsory Service	Population in Services %
Argentina	180,500	★	0.6
Australia	73,200		0.5
Canada	82,900	★	0.3
Egypt	452,000	★	1.1
France	492,000	★	0.9
Netherlands	104,000	★	0.7
New Zealand	12,900		0.4
Sweden	64,500	★	0.8
South Africa	81,400	★	0.3
UK	327,600		0.6

Medals

The awarding of medals is comparatively modern. Soldiers weren't really interested in honours. What they wanted was their share of the plunder. It was the Greeks who first awarded laurel wreaths to successful competitors in the Olympic Games. The Romans adopted the awarding of laurel wreaths; but instead of giving them to sportsmen, they gave them to successful soldiers.

The first medals struck in this country were the Armada medals, oval discs meant to be hung round the neck, and they were given by Elizabeth I to commanders of ships who had contributed to the defeat of the Spanish Armada.

The first mass distribution of medals was ordered by a relieved Parliament to all those who had taken part in the battle of Dunbar in 1650. It wasn't repeated until the issue of the Waterloo medals to all those who had taken part in the battle in 1815, and these weren't actually given out until 1848.

Medals and Honours		Instituted	Awarded
Victoria Cross	(VC)	1856	to members of the services, staff of nursing services and civilians under the orders of the military; the highest award for all ranks
George Cross	(GC)	1940	for acts of conspicuous bravery in extreme danger; the highest award for civilians
Distinguished Service Order	(DSO)	1886	for special services to commissioned officers of the services and the merchant navy
Distinguished Service Cross	(DSC)	1914	to RN officers below the rank of captain, and to warrant officers
Military Cross	(MC)	1914	to army officers below the rank of captain and to warrant officers
Distinguished Flying Cross	(DFC)	1918	to RAF officers and warrant officers when engaged in wartime operations
Air Force Cross	(AFC)	1918	to RAF officers and warrant officers for courage when flying, but not during wartime operations
Albert Medal	(AM)	1866	for gallantry in saving life at sea

Medals and Honours		Instituted	Awarded
Medal for Distinguished Conduct in the Field	(DCM)	1954	to warrant officers, non-commissioned officers, and men in the army and the RAF
Conspicuous Gallantry Medal	(CGM)	1874	to warrant officers and men of the RN, the RAF and the merchant navy
George Medal	(GM)	1940	for gallantry, frequently awarded to civilians
Edward Medal	(EM)	1907	to miners or quarrymen who have risked their lives in rescuing others
Distinguished Service Medal	(DSM)	1914	to chief petty officers and below, of all branches of the RN and merchant navy and to non-commissioned officers and men of the Royal Marines
Military Medal	(MM)	1916	to warrant, and non-commissioned officers
Distinguished Flying Medal	(DFM)	1914	to warrant officers and below in the RAF and the Fleet Air Arm

8 THE ARTS

Since life was nothing but a long hard struggle for survival, it is remarkable that early in his development, man recorded life around him in cave paintings and primitive sculptures.

He probably used some form of drum very early on, since it was the most effective way of conveying a message or warning over a long distance, but he also made other musical instruments. Whistles and flutes dating from 25,000 BC have been found in Hungary and the USSR, and a Sumerian clay tablet inscribed with a musical notation, and dated about 1,800 BC, has been unearthed in Iraq.

People made up prayers and spells for rituals, and they must have told stories and, as soon as a written language was invented, recorded them. Poets and playwrights were part of the courts of the early civilizations, and by 1,000 BC there were public theatres, crowded with people watching actors and dancers and listening to the musicians who accompanied their performances.

Masters of the King's/Queen's Musick

The English have always been music lovers. King Henry VIII wrote music, some of which still exists, and Queen Elizabeth I was a talented performer on the virginals, an early keyboard instrument.

Although there were always musicians at court, Charles I decided to employ someone whose job it would be to provide music on special occasions and so, in 1626, he appointed Nicholas Lanier as the Master of the King's Musick. Then came the Civil War and the execution of the King, and the post was abolished, but after the Restoration, Charles II reinstated Nicholas Lanier. Since then, there have been eighteen Masters of the King's Musick.

Name	Lived	Appointed	Monarch
Nicholas Lanier	1588–1666	1626	Charles I, Charles II
Louis Grabu	c. 1638–94	1666	Charles II

Name	Lived	Appointed	Monarch
Nicholas Staggins	? –1700	1674	Charles II, James II, William and Mary, William III
John Eccles	1668–1735	1700	Anne, George I, George II
Maurice Green	1695–1755	1735	George II
William Boyce	1710–79	1757	George II, George III
John Stanley	1713–86	1772	George III
Sir William Parsons	1746–1817	1786	George III
William Shield	1748–1829	1817	George III, George IV
Christian Kramer	c.1788–1848	1829	George IV, William IV, Victoria
François Cramer	1772–1848	1834	Victoria
George Anderson	1801–76	1848	Victoria
Sir William Cusins	1833–93	1870	Victoria
Sir Walter Parratt	1841–1924	1893	Victoria, Edward VII, George V
Sir Edward Elgar	1857–1934	1924	George V
Sir Henry Walford Davies	1869–1941	1934	George V, Edward VIII, George VI
Sir Arnold Bax	1883–1953	1941	George VI, Elizabeth II
Sir Arthur Bliss	1891–1973	1953	Elizabeth II
Sir Malcolm Williamson	1931	1975	Elizabeth II

The Orchestra

For a long time orchestras were simply known as bands. Whoever used the word 'orchestra' went back to the Greeks, but got it wrong. In Ancient Greece, the orchestra was actually the space between the stage and the audience where dances were sometimes performed to the accompaniment of instruments.

Orchestras of the World

Name	Date Formed
Amsterdam Concertgebouw	1882 (first concert 1888)
Berlin Philharmonic	1882
Boston Symphony	1881
BBC Symphony	1930
Chicago Symphony	1886
Cincinatti Symphony	1894
City of Birmingham Symphony	1916
Cleveland Symphony	1918
Czech Philharmonic	1894 (first concert 1896)
Gewandhaus	1780
Hallé	1858
Lamoureux	1881
Liverpool Philharmonic	1842
London Philharmonic	1932
London Symphony	1904
Los Angeles Symphony	1896
Minneapolis Symphony	1903
Moscow Philharmonic	1864
Munich Philharmonic	1893
New Philharmonia	1964
New York Philharmonic Symphony	1842
Orchestre de Paris	1967
Orchestre de la Suisse Romande	1918
Philadelphia	1900
Philharmonia	1945
Pittsburg Symphony	1899
St Louis Symphony	1907
Société des Concerts du Conservatoire	1828
Vienna Philharmonic	1842
Warsaw Philharmonic	1901

The Instruments of an Orchestra

The type and number of instruments needed for a particular concert vary. The instruments listed below are those which are constantly in use.

Instrument	French Name	German Name	Italian
Brass:			
horn	cor	Horn	corno
trombone	trombone	Posaune	trombone
trumpet	trompette	Trompete	tromba
tuba	tuba	Tuba (Basstuba)	tuba
Percussion:			
bass drum	grosse caisse	Grosse Trommel	gran casa
cymbals	cymbals	Becken	piatti (cinelli)
kettle drum	timbales	Pauken	timpani
side drum	tambour militaire (caisse claire)	Kleine Trommel	tamburo militaire
triangle	triangle	Triangel	triangolo
Strings:			
cello	violoncelle	Violoncell	violoncello
double bass	contra basse	Kontrabass	contrabasso
harp	harpe	Harfe	arpa
viola	alto	Bratsche	viola
violin	violon	Violine (Geige)	violino
Woodwind:			
bassoon	basson	Fagott	fagotto
clarinet	clarinette	Klarinette	clarinetto
double bassoon	contra basson	Kontrafagott	contrafagotto
English horn	cor Anglais	Englisches Horn	corno inglese
flute	flûte	Flöte	flauto
piccolo	petit flûte	Kleine Flöte	flauto piccolo (ottavino)
oboe	hautbois	Hoboe (Oboe)	oboe

- Norway holds the world's record for the biggest orchestra ever assembled: 20,100 people took part in 1964.
- Johann Strauss the Younger conducted an orchestra of 987 pieces and a choir of 20,000 in Boston, USA in 1872.

Some Other Instruments

Name	Description
euphonium	tenor tuba in B flat with a more mellow tone than the tuba; used mainly in brass bands; invented c. 1840
celesta	small keyboard instrument with clear bell-like tones produced by the striking of hammers against small metal plates; invented c. 1880
piano	percussion instrument with each of the keys of the keyboard operating a small felt-covered hammer which strikes a corresponding steel wire; invented c. 1710, iron-framed piano c. 1860
lute	stringed instrument with a body shaped like half a pear with six to thirteen strings stretched along the fretted neck (which is sometimes bent to form a sharp angle); in use for thousands of years throughout the world
tambourine	shallow hand-drum consisting of one head with metal discs around the rim; when hit with the knuckle or shaken, the discs jingle; in use in Roman times

Composers

Composers	Lived	Country
Arne, Thomas Augustin	1710–78	UK
Bach, Johann Sebastian	1685–1750	Germany
Bartók, Béla	1881–1945	Hungary
Beethoven, Ludwig Van	1770–1827	Germany
Bellini, Vincenzo	1801–35	Italy
Berlioz, Hector	1803–69	France
Boccherini, Luigi	1743–1805	Italy
Borodin, Alexander	1833–87	Russia
Brahms, Johannes	1833–97	Germany
Britten, Benjamin	1913–84	UK
Bruckner, Anton	1824–96	Austria
Chabrier, Emmanuel	1841–94	France
Chopin, Frédérick	1810–49	Poland
Clarke, Jeremiah	1659–1707	UK
Copland, Aaron	1900–	USA

Composers	Lived	Country
Debussy, Claude	1862–1918	France
Delibes, Léo	1836–91	France
Delius, Frederick	1863–1934	UK
Dickinson, Clarence	1873–1967	USA
Donizetti, Gaetano	1797–1848	Italy
Elgar, Sir Edward	1857–1934	UK
Franck, César Auguste	1822–90	Belgium
German, Sir Edward	1862–1936	UK
Glinka, Mikhail Ivanovitch	1804–57	Russia
Grenados, Enrique	1867–1916	Spain
Handel, George Frederick	1685–1759	Germany (UK 1726)
Haydn, Franz Joseph	1732–1809	Austria
Hindemith, Paul	1895–1963	Germany
Hoffman, Ernst Theodor	1776–1822	Germany
Holst, Gustav Theodore	1874–1934	UK
Humperdinck, Engelbert	1854–1921	Germany
Ives, Charles	1874–1954	USA
Janaćěk, Leoš	1854–1928	Czechoslovakia
Liszt, Franz	1811–86	Hungary
Lully, Jean-Baptiste	1632–87	Italy (France 1661)
Mahler, Gustav	1860–1911	Austria
Mendelssohn, Jakob Ludwig	1809–47	Germany
Mozart, Wolfgang Amadeus	1756–91	Austria
Mussorgsky, Modest Petrovitch	1839–81	Russia
Nielsen, Carl August	1865–1931	Denmark
Offenbach, Jacques	1819–80	Germany
Palestrina, Giovanni Pierluigi	1743–1803	Italy
Poulenc, Francis	1899–1963	France
Prokoviev, Serge	1891–1953	Russia
Puccini, Giacomo	1858–1924	Italy
Rachmaninov, Sergei	1873–1943	Russia
Respighi, Ottorino	1879–1936	Italy
Rossini, Gioachino	1792–1868	Italy
Saint-Saëns, Camille	1835–1921	France
Schoenberg, Arnold	1874–1951	Austria
Schubert, Franz Peter	1797–1828	Austria
Schumann, Robert	1810–56	Germany
Sibelius, Jean	1865–1957	Finland

Composers	Lived	Country
Smetana, Fredrich	1824–84	Czechoslovakia
Straus, Oscar	1870–1954	Austria
Strauss, Johann	1825–99	Austria
Strauss, Richard	1864–1949	Germany
Stravinsky, Igor	1882–1971	Russia (USA 1945)
Sullivan, Sir Arthur	1842–1900	UK
Tchaikovsky, Peter Ilyich	1840–93	Russia
Verdi, Guiseppe	1813–1901	Italy
Wagner, Richard	1813–83	Germany
Warlock, Peter	1894–1930	UK
Weill, Kurt	1900–50	Germany
Wolf, Hugo	1860–1903	Austria

o 64 members of the Bach family were either professional composers or performers in the years between 1600 and 1800.
o The most prolific composer was Telemann, but a full count of his compositions has not yet been completed.
o Mozart composed over 1,000 pieces of music before he died at the age of 35. His earliest work was written when he was four years old.

Some Musical Terms

Term	Meaning
adagio	slow, but faster than largo
agitato	excited
allegretto	light and cheerful, between allegro and andante in tempo
allegro	lively, brisk
andante	flowing, peaceful
andantino	slightly slower than andante
appassionato	intense, passionate
aria	song or tune, usually for a single voice
baritone	male voice between tenor and bass
brillante	sparkling, brilliant
brio	vigorous, fiery
contralto	female voice, the lowest register
crescendo	gradually increasing in tone

Term	Meaning
dolce	sweetly, softly
dolente	sadly, pathetically
finale	final part or movement
forte	loud, strong
fortissimo	very loud, very strong
grave	serious, slow, majestic
intermezzo	interlude
largo	slow, solemn, dignified
lento	slow
mesto	melancholic
mezzo soprano	female voice between soprano and contralto
moderato	moderate
molto	much
pianissimo	very quiet, soft
piano	quiet
pizzicato	plucking of strings
presto	fast
recitative	declamatory singing
reprise	repeat
rhythm	measured time
ritenuto	sudden slowing of tempo
scherzo	lively piece
soprano	female voice, highest range
sotto voce	half the voice
tenor	male voice, highest range
timbre	quality of tone
tosto	quick, swift
tranquillo	tranquil, quiet
tutti	all
virtuoso	performer with remarkable expertise
vivace	lively, briskly

Literature

When men had to write everything by hand, very few copies were made of any manuscript. It took a long time, and not very many people knew how to read and write.

It was the invention of the printing press that marked a big step forward in literacy. The first book was printed in China in 853, and by 1045 the Chinese had invented moveable type printing. It wasn't until 1445 that Johannes Gutenberg printed the first book in Europe, and in 1474 William Caxton printed the first book in English.

Some Children's Authors

Although children were taught nursery rhymes and told stories, it was a long time before books were specially written for them.

Some Children's Authors	Lived	Country	Well-known Title
Alcott, Louisa May	1832–88	USA	*Little Women*
Andersen, Hans Christian	1805–75	Denmark	fairy tales
Ballantyne, Robert	1825–94	UK	*Coral Island*
Barrie, Sir James	1860–1937	UK	*Peter Pan*
Blyton, Enid	1897–1968	UK	*The Famous Five*
Burnett, Frances Hodgson	1849–1924	UK	*The Secret Garden*
Carroll, Lewis (Charles Dodgson)	1832–95	UK	*Alice's Adventures in Wonderland*
Grahame, Kenneth	1859–1932	UK	*The Wind in the Willows*
Kipling, Rudyard	1865–1936	UK	*Just So Stories*
Milne, Alan Alexander	1882–1956	UK	*Winnie the Pooh*
Nesbit, Edith	1858–1924	UK	*The Railway Children*
Perrault, Charles	1628–1703	France	*Cinderella*, and other other fairy tales
Potter, Beatrix	1866–1943	UK	*Peter Rabbit*
Ransome, Arthur	1884–1967	UK	*Swallows and Amazons*
Sewell, Anna	1820–78	UK	*Black Beauty*
Stevenson, Robert Louis	1850–94	UK	*Treasure Island*
Twain, Mark	1835–1910	USA	*The Adventures of Tom Sawyer*

Dramatists

Dramatist	Lived	Country	Well-known Title
Aeschylus	c. 525–456 BC	Greece	*The Persians*
Albee, Edward	1928–	USA	*Who's Afraid of Virginia Woolf?*
Anouilh, Jean	1910–	France	*Ring Round the Moon*
Aristophanes	c. 448–380 BC	Greece	*Birds*
Beckett, Samuel	1906–	Ireland	*Waiting for Godot*
Brecht, Bertolt	1898–1955	Germany	*Mother Courage*
Capek, Karel	1890–1938	Czechoslovakia	*The Insect Play*
Chekhov, Anton	1860–1904	Russia	*Uncle Vanya*
Cocteau, Jean	1891–1963	France	*Orphée*
Corneille, Pierre	1606–84	France	*Le Menteur*
Euripides	c. 484–407 BC	Greece	*Electra*
Farquhar, George	1677–1707	Ireland	*The Beaux' Straagem*
Fry, Christopher	1907–	UK	*The Lady's Not for Burning*
Ibsen, Henrik	1828–1906	Norway	*Hedda Gabler*
Jonson, Ben	1572–1637	UK	*Volpone*
Marlowe, Christopher	1564-93	UK	*Edward II*
Miller, Arthur	1915–	USA	*The Crucible*
Molière (Poquelin, Jean Baptiste)	1622–73	France	*Le Bourgeois Gentilhomme*
O'Casey, Sean	1884–1964	Ireland	*The Plough and the Stars*
O'Neill, Eugene	1888–1953	USA	*The Iceman Cometh*
Pinter, Harold	1930–	UK	*The Caretaker*
Pirandello, Luigi	1867–1936	Italy	*Six Characters in Search of an Author*
Shakespeare, William	1564–1616	UK	1589-93 *Titus Andronicus* *The Comedy of Errors* *The Taming of the Shrew*

Dramatist	Lived	Country	Well-known Title
Shakespeare, William			*Two Gentlemen of Verona*
			Henry VI (Part I)
			Henry VI (Part II)
			Henry VI (Part III)
			Richard III
			Love's Labours Lost
			1594–5
			Romeo and Juliet
			Midsummer Night's Dream
			Richard II
			1596
			King John
			Merchant of Venice
			1597–9
			Henry IV (Part I)
			Henry IV (Part II)
			Henry V
			The Merry Wives of Windsor
			Much Ado about Nothing
			As You Like It
			Twelfth Night
			Julius Caesar
			1601–4
			Troilus and Cressida
			All's Well that Ends Well
			Measure for Measure
			Hamlet
			1604–6
			Othello
			Macbeth
			King Lear
			Timon of Athens

Dramatist	Lived	Country	Well-known Title
Shakespeare, William			1607–8 *Anthony and Cleopatra* *Coriolanus* 1608–11 *Pericles* *Cymbeline* *The Winter's Tale* *The Tempest* 1613 *Henry VIII*
Shaw, George Bernard	1856–1950	Ireland	*Pygmalion*
Sherwood, Robert	1896–1955	USA	*The Petrified Forest*
Sophocles	495–406 BC	Greece	*King Oedipus*
Synge, John Millington	1871–1909	Ireland	*Playboy of the Western World*
Turgenev, Ivan	1818–83	Russia	*A Month in the Country*
Wilde, Oscar	1854–1900	Ireland	*The Importance of Being Earnest*
Williams, Tennessee	1911–83	USA	*The Glass Menagerie*

Writers

Some Important American Writers

Writer	Lived	Type of Work
Allen, Hervey	1889–1949	novelist, poet, biographer
Baldwin, James	1924–	novelist, playwright, essayist
Bellow, Saul	1915–	novelist
Benchley, Robert	1889–1945	novelist, humourist
Bradbury, Ray	1920–	novelist (science fiction)
Cooper, James Fenimore	1789–1851	novelist
Dreiser, Theodore	1871–1945	novelist
Faulkner, William	1897–1962	novelist
Fitzgerald, Francis Scott	1896–1940	novelist

Writer	Lived	Type of Work
Hawthorne, Nathaniel	1804–64	novelist, short stories
Hemingway, Ernest	1898–1961	novelist
Irving, Washington	1783–1859	novelist, biographer
James, Henry	1843–1916	novelist
Lewis, Sinclair	1885–1951	novelist
Mailer, Norman	1923–	novelist
Parker, Dorothy	1893–1967	short stories, poet
Poe, Edgar Allan	1809–49	novelist (supernatural), poet
Salinger, J. D.	1919–	novelist
Steinbeck, John	1902–68	novelist
Twain, Mark	1835–1910	novelist, humourist
Thurber, James	1894–1961	short stories, humourist

Some Important British Writers

Writer	Lived	Type of Work
Addison, Joseph	1672–1719	essayist, poet
Amis, Kingsley	1922–	novelist
Austin, Jane	1755–1817	novelist
Bacon, Francis	1561–1626	essayist
Bennett, Arnold	1867–1631	novelist, playwright
Boswell, James	1740–95	diarist, biographer
Brontë, Anne	1820–49	novelist, poet
Brontë, Charlotte	1816–55	novelist, poet
Brontë, Emily	1818–48	novelist, poet
Buchan, John (Lord Tweedsmuir)	1829–1907	novelist (adventure thrillers)
Conrad, Joseph	1857–1924	novelist (sea stories)
Dickens, Charles	1812–70	novelist
Doyle, Sir Arthur Conan	1859–1930	novelist (detective stories)
Eliot, George (Evans, Mary Anne)	1819–80	novelist
Evelyn, John	1620–1706	diarist
Fielding, Henry	1707–52	novelist
Forester, Cecil Scott	1899–1966	novelist (sea stories)
Forster, Edward Morgan	1879–1970	novelist
Galsworthy, John	1867–1933	novelist, playwright
Gibbon, Edward	1737–94	historian

Writer	Lived	Type of Work
Golding, William	1911–	novelist
Graves, Robert	1895–1986	novelist, poet
Greene, Grahame	1904–	novelist
Haggard, Sir Henry Rider	1856–1925	novelist (adventure stories)
Hardy, Thomas	1840–1928	novelist, poet
Hazlitt, William	1778–1830	essayist
Huxley, Aldous	1894–1963	novelist, essayist
Johnson, Samuel	1709–84	novelist, critic, lexicographer
Lamb, Charles	1775–1834	essayist
Laski, Marghanita	1915–	novelist, critic, playwright
Lawrence, David Herbert	1885–1930	novelist, poet
Lehmann, Rosamund	1904–	novelist
Macaulay, Thomas Babington	1800–59	historian, essayist, poet
Maugham, William Somerset	1874–1965	novelist, short stories, playwright
Morgan, Charles	1894–1958	novelist
Orwell, George	1903–50	novelist
Pepys, Samuel	1633–1703	diarist
Priestley, John Boynton	1894–1984	novelist, playwright
Saki (Munro, Hugh Hector)	1870–1916	short stories, novelist
Scott, Sir Walter	1771–1832	novelist
Sillitoe, Alan	1928–	novelist
Thackeray, William Makepeace	1811–63	novelist
Waugh, Evelyn	1903–66	novelist
Wells, Herbert George	1866–1946	novelist
Wilson, Colin	1931–	novelist

Some Important French Writers

Writer	Lived	Type of Work
Balzac, Honoré de	1799–1850	novelist
Beavoir, Simone de	1908–	novelist
Camus, Albert	1913–60	novelist, essayist
Daudet, Alphonse	1840–97	novelist

Writer	Lived	Type of Work
Dumas, Alexandre	1802–70	novelist
France, Anatole	1844–1924	novelist, poet, critic
Gide, André	1869–1951	novelist
Hugo, Victor	1902–85	novelist, playwright, poet
Maupassant, Guy de	1850–93	novelist, short stories
Montaigne, Michel	1533–92	essayist
Proust, Marcel	1871–1922	novelist
Sartre, Jean Paul	1905–80	playwright, novelist, essayist
Voltaire (François Marie Arouet)	1694–1778	playwright, poet, novelist
Zola, Emile	1840–1902	novelist

Some Important Russian Writers

Writer	Lived	Type of Work
Dostoevsky, Fyodor	1821–81	novelist
Gogol, Nicolai	1809–52	novelist
Gorky, Maxim	1868–1936	novelist, playwright
Pasternak, Boris	1890–1960	novelist, poet
Pushkin, Alexander	1799–1837	poet, novelist
Solzhenitsyn, Alexander	1918–	novelist
Tolstoy, Leo	1828–1910	novelist

Some Other Important Writers

Writer	Lived	Country
Boccaccio, Giovanni	1313–75	Italy
Cervantes, Miguel	1547–1616	Spain
Joyce, James	1882–1941	Ireland
Kafka, Franz	1883–1941	Czechoslovakia
Mann, Thomas	1875–1955	Germany
Naipul, Vidiadhur	1932–	India (Trinidad-born)
Paton, Alan	1903–	South Africa
White, Patrick	1912–	Australia

Poets

Poet	Lived	Country
Alcaeus	c. 611–580	Greece
Betjeman, John	1906–84	UK
Blake, William	1757–1827	UK
Blunt, William	1840–1922	UK
Bridges, Robert	1844–1930	UK
Brooke, Rupert	1887–1915	UK
Browning, Robert	1812–89	UK
Burns, Robert	1759–96	UK
Byron, George	1788–1824	UK
Campion, Thomas	1567–1620	UK
Catullus, Gaius	c. 84–54	Roman
Chaucer, Geoffrey	c. 1340–1400	UK
Coleridge, Samuel Taylor	1772–1834	UK
De La Mare, Walter	1873–1953	UK
Donne, John	1571–1631	UK
Drinkwater, John	1882–1937	UK
Dryden, John	1631–1700	UK
Eliot, Thomas Stearns	1888–1965	UK/USA
Flecker, James Elroy	1884–1915	UK
Frost, Robert	1874–1963	USA
Gautier, Théophile	1811–72	France
Goethe, Johann	1749–1834	Germany
Goldsmith, Oliver	1728–74	Ireland
Herrick, Robert	1591–1674	UK
Hopkins, Gerard Manley	1844–89	UK
Housman, Alfred	1859–89	UK
Keats, John	1795–1821	UK
Larkin, Philip	1922–85	UK
Leopardi, Giacomo	1798–1837	Italy
Longfellow, Henry Wadsworth	1807–82	USA
Mallarmé, Stéphane	1842–98	France
Marvell, Andrew	1621–78	UK
Milton, John	1608–74	UK
Pope, Alexander	1688–1744	UK
Pound, Ezra	1885–1972	USA
Sandburg, Carl	1878–1967	USA
Shelley, Percy Bysshe	1792–1822	UK
Tennyson, Alfred Lord	1809–1902	UK

Poet	Lived	Country
Thomas, Dylan	1914–53	UK
Villon, François	1431–85	France
Wordsworth, William	1770–1850	UK
Yeats, William Butler	1865–1939	Ireland

Poets Laureate

The Poet Laureate is a poet who is attached to the royal household and who is expected to write verse to commemorate important occasions. The position of the first three poets was unofficial; John Dryden was the first official Poet Laureate.

Name	Lived	Appointed	Monarch
Samuel Daniel	1562–1619	1599	Elizabeth I, James I
Ben Jonson	1572–1637	1619	James I, Charles I
Sir William D'Avenant	1606–68	1637	Charles I, Charles II
John Dryden	1631–1700	1668	Charles II, James II
Thomas Shadwell	1642–92	1689	William and Mary
Nahum Tate	1652–1715	1692	William and Mary, Anne, George I
Nicholas Rowe	1674–1718	1715	George I
Laurence Eusden	1688–1730	1718	George I, George II
Colley Cibber	1671–1757	1730	George II
William Whitehead	1715–85	1757	George II, George III
Rev Thomas Warton	1728–90	1785	George III
Henry James Pye	1745–1813	1790	George III
Robert Southey	1774–1843	1813	George III, George IV, William IV, Victoria
William Wordsworth	1770–1850	1843	Victoria
Alfred, Lord Tennyson	1809–92	1850	Victoria
Alfred Austin	1835–1913	1896	Victoria, Edward VII, George V
Robert Bridges	1844–1930	1913	George V
John Masefield	1878–1967	1930	George V, Edward VIII, George VI, Elizabeth II

Name	Lived	Appointed	Monarch
Cecil Day Lewis	1904–72	1967	Elizabeth II
Sir John Betjeman	1906–84	1972	Elizabeth II
Edward (Ted) Hughes	1930–	1984	Elizabeth II

Artists

American Artists: Eighteenth and Nineteenth Centuries

Name	Lived	Name	Lived
Allston, Washington	1779–1843	Morse, Samuel	1791–1870
Bingham, George	1811–79	Pealle, Charles Willson	1741–1827
Cassatt, Mary	1844–1926		
Cole, Thomas	1801–48	Peto, John	1854–1907
Davies, Arthur	1862–1928	Ryder, Albert	1847–1917
Durand, Asher	1796–1886	Sully, Thomas	1783–1872
Earl, Ralph	1751–1801	Trimbull, John	1756–1843
Harnett, William	1848–92	West, Benjamin	1738–1820
Homer, Winslow	1836–1910	Whistler, James	1834–1903
Innes, George	1825–94		

British Artists: Sixteenth to Nineteenth Centuries

Artist	Lived	Artist	Lived
Blake, William	1757–1827	Leighton, Frederick Lord	1830–96
Constable, John	1776–1837		
Cotman, John	1782–1842	Lely, Sir Peter	1618–80
Etty, William	1787–1849	Morland, George	c. 1762–1804
Gainsborough, Thomas	1727–88	Palmer, Samuel	1805–81
		Raeburn, Sir Henry	1756–1823
Hilliard, Nicholas	c. 1547–1619	Reynolds, Sir Joshua	1723–92
Hogarth, William	1697–1764	Stubbs, George	1724–1806
Kneller, Sir Godfrey	1646–1723	Turner, Joseph William Mallard	1775–1851
Landseer, Sir Edwin	1802–73		
Lawrence, Sir Thomas	1769–1830	Watts, George	1817–1904

French Artists: Seventeenth to Nineteenth Centuries

Artist	Lived	Artist	Lived
Boucher, François	1703–70	Fragonard, Jean	1732–1806
Chardin, Jean	1699–1779	Gellée, Claude	1600–82
Corot, Jean	1796–1875	Greuze, Jean	1725–1805
Courbet, Gustav	1819–77	Ingres, Jean	1780–1867
David, Jacques	1748–1825	Mercier, Georges	1763–1843
Daumier, Honoré	1808–79	Prud'hon, Pierre	1758–1823
Delacroix, Eugène	1798–1863	Watteau, Jean	1684–1823

Flemish/Dutch Artists: Fifteenth to Eighteenth Centuries

Artist	Lived	Artist	Lived
Bosch, Hierongmus	c. 1450–1516	Lievens, Jan	1607–74
Brueghel, Pieter	c. 1525–69	Rembrandt van Ryn	1609–69
Cuyp, Alebert	1620–91	Rubens, Sir Peter Paul	1577–1640
Dyck, Sir Anthony van	1599–1641	Ruisdael, Jacob van	c. 1628–82
Eyck, Jan van	c. 1390–1441	Steen, Jan	c. 1625–79
Goyen, Jan van	1596–1656	Teniers, David (III)	1638–85
Hals, Frans	c. 1581–1688	Vermeer, Jan	1632–75
Heyden, Jan van der	1637–1712	Witte, Emanuel de	c. 1615–1692
Holbein, Hans	c. 1497–1543		

Italian Artists: Fifteenth to Eighteenth Centuries

Artist	Lived	
Andrea del Sarto	1486–1530	Florence
Angelico, Fra	c. 1387–1455	Florence
Bartelommea della Porto, Fra	c. 1475–1517	Florence
Bellini, Jacobo	c. 1400–70	Venice
Bellini, Giovanni	c. 1430–1516	Venice
Botticelli, Sandro	c. 1445–1510	Florence
Canaletto, Antonio	c. 1697–1768	Venice

Artist	Lived	
Caracciolo, Goivanni	1578–1635	Naples
Caravaggio, Michelangelo	1571–1610	Milan
Correggio, Antonio	c. 1494–1534	Parma
Gérard, Baron François	1770–1837	Rome
Giorgione	c. 1476–1510	Venice
Michelangelo Buonarroti	1475–1564	Florence
Raphael Sanzio	1483–1520	Rome
Tintoretto	1518–94	Venice
Titian	c. 1487–1576	Venice
Veronese, Paoli	c. 1528–88	Venice
Vinci, Leonardo da	1452–1519	Milan

German Artists: Fifteenth to Nineteenth Centuries

Artist	Lived	Artist	Lived
Bonheur, Rosa	1822–99	Friedrich, Caspar	1774–1840
Bruyn, Barthel	c. 1471–1528	Grünewald, Matthias	
Claesz, Pieter	c. 1598–1660		c. 1470–1528
Durer, Albrecht	1471–1528	Hackert, Philipp	1737–1807
Elsheimer, Adam	1578–1610	Pencz, Georg	c. 1500–50

Spanish Artists: Fifteenth to Nineteenth Centuries

Artist	Lived	Artist	Lived
Antolínez, José	1635–75	Melendez, Louis	1716–80
Berruguete, Pedro	c. 1450–1503	Moreles, Luis	c. 1530–86
El Greco (Theotocopouli,		Murillo, Bartolomé	c. 1617–82
Doménico)	1541–1614	Velasquez, Diego de	
Goya, Francisco	1746–1828	Silva y	1599–1660

Special Groups of Nineteenth and Twentieth-Century Artists

There have always been groups of painters who know each other well and influence each other's work, but this was particularly true during the late nineteenth and twentieth century. Sometimes it is difficult to put artists in specific categories. Cézanne, for example, contributed to the first Impressionist exhibition, moved away from the Impressionists and later influenced the emerging Cubists.

Pre-Raphaelites

Artist	Lived	Country
Brown, Ford Madox	1821–93	UK
Burne-Jones, Sir Edward	1833–98	UK
Hunt, William Holman	1827–1910	UK
Millais, Sir John	1829–96	UK
Rossetti, Dante Gabriel	1828–82	UK

Impressionists

Artist	Lived	Country
Cassatt, Mary	1844–1926	USA
Degas, Hilaire	1834–1917	France
Libermann, Max	1847–1935	German
Manet, Edouard	1832–83	France
Monet, Claude	1840–1926	France
Morisot, Berthe	1841–95	France
Pisarro, Camille	1830–1903	France
Renoir, Pierre Auguste	1841–1919	France
Sisley, Alfred	1840–99	UK

Post Impressionists

Artist	Lived	Country
Cézanne, Paul	1839–1906	France
Gauguin, Paul	1848–1903	France
Toulouse-Lautrec, Henri	1864–1901	France
Van Gogh, Vincent	1853–90	Holland

Fauvists

Artist	Lived	Country
Derain, André	1880–1954	France
Dufy, Raoul	1877–1953	France
Matisse, Henri	1869–1953	France

Cubists

Artist	Lived	Country
Braque, Georges	1882–1963	France
Delaunay, Robert	1855–1941	France
Gris, Juan	1887–1927	Spain
Picasso, Pablo	1881–1973	Spain/France

Surrealists

Artist	Lived	Country
Dali, Salvador	1905–	Spain
Ernst, Max	1891–1976	Germany
Miró, Joan	1893–1983	Spain
Tanguy, Yves	1900–55	France

Other Important Late Nineteenth and Twentieth-Century Artists

Artist	Lived	Country
Bacon, Francis	1909–	UK
Boyd, Arthur	1920–	Australia
Bratby, John	1928–	UK
Carr, Emily	1871–1945	Canada
Dobell, William	1897–1970	Australia
Dongen, Kees van	1877–1968	Holland
Drysdale, Sir Russell	1912–81	Australia
Ensor, James	1860–1949	Belgium
Hodgkins, Frances	1869–1947	New Zealand
John, Augustus	1878–1961	UK
Johns, Jasper	1930–	USA

Artist	Lived	Country
Kitaj, R. B.	1932–	USA
Kleè, Paul	1879–1940	Switzerland
Lewis, Wyndham	1884–1957	UK
Lichtenstein, Roy	1923–	USA
Lowry, L. S.	1887–1976	UK
Modigliani, Amedeo	1884–1920	Italy
Mondrian, Piet	1872–1944	Holland
Nash, Paul	1889–1946	UK
Nicholson, Ben	1894–1982	UK
Nolan, Sir Sidney	1917–	Australia
Nolde, Emil	1867–1956	Germany
Oldenburg, Claes	1929–	USA
Pasmore, Victor	1908–	UK
Riley, Bridget	1931–	UK
Rivera, Diego	1886–1957	Mexico
Portinari, Cándido	1903–63	Brazil
Richards, Ceri	1903–71	UK
Riopelle, Jean Paul	1923–	Canada
Spencer, Sir Stanley	1891–1959	UK
Vasarély, Victor	1908–	France
Warhol, Andy	1928–	USA
Yeats, Jack	1871–1957	Ireland

Some Important Sculptors

Sculptor	Lived	Country
Barye, Antoine-Louis	1796–1875	France
Bernini, Gianlorenzo	1598–1680	Italy
Bologna, Giovanni	1529–1608	Italy
Butler, Reg	1913–81	UK
Canova, Antonio	1757–1822	Italy
Capeaux, Jean	1827–75	France
Cellini, Benvenuto	1500–71	Italy
Chadwick, Lynn	1914–	UK
Donatello	1386–1466	Italy
Epstein, Sir Jacob	1880–1959	UK
González, Julio	1876–1942	Spain
Hepworth, Barbara	1903–75	UK
Manzü, Giacomo	1908–	Italy

Sculptor	Lived	Country
Milles, Carl	1875–1955	Sweden
Michelangelo Buonarotti	1475–1564	Italy
Moore, Henry	1898–1986	UK
Quercia, Jacopo della	c. 1374–1438	Italy
Richier, Germaine	1904–59	France
Rodin, Auguste	1840–1917	France
Sergel, Johan Tobias von	1740–1814	Sweden

9 SCIENCE AND MATHEMATICS

Inventions and Discoveries

We usually know who invented what during the last two or three hundred years or so, although there are still some unresolved disputes since, occasionally, people in different countries were working on similar projects at the same time, and each claimed to be first. Today, as machines become more complex, it is seldom that one person is responsible for any one invention. Usually, it is the result of a team effort.

Invention/Discovery	Name	Date
adding machine	B Pascal (Fr)	1612
air brake	G Westinghouse (USA)	1868
air conditioning	W Carrier (USA)	1911
barometer	E Torricelli (It)	1643
bifocal lens	B Franklin (USA)	1780
bobbin-net machine	J Heathcoat (UK)	1809
calculating machine	C Babbage (UK)	1835
camera	J Niepce (Fr)	1822
camera, roll film	G Eastman (UK)	1884
carding machine	J Hargreaves (UK)	1760
cash registar	J Ritty (USA)	1879
cathode ray tube (commercial use)	K Braun (Ger)	1897
cement	L Vicat (Fr)	1824
cement, Portland	J Aspdin (UK)	1824
cinema (patented)	W Friese-Greene (UK)	1889
cinema, first public showing	France	1895
clock, electric	M Hipp (Ger)	1842
clock, mechanical	I'Hsing and Liang Ling-tsan (Chi)	725
clock, pendulum	C Huygens (Neth)	1657
coal-gas lighting	W Murdock (UK)	1792
computer	unknown (Greece)	80 BC

Invention/Discovery	Name	Date
computer, first programmable	M Newman (formulated), T Flowers (built) (UK)	1943
computer, micro	M Hoff Jr (USA)	1969–73
crossword	A Wynn (USA)	1831
dynamite	A Nobel (Swe)	1867
dynamo	M Faraday (UK)	1831
electric lamp	T Edison (USA)	1860
electromagnetic motor	J Henry (USA)	1829
engine, steam (patented)	Captain Savory (UK)	1689
engine, atmospheric	T Newcomen (UK)	1705
engine, steam turbine	Sir C Parsons (UK)	1889
gear, differential	C Pecquer (Fr)	1828
gramophone (phonograph)	T Edison (USA)	1878
gyrocompass	E Sperry (USA)	1911
gyroscope	J Foucault (Fr)	1851
identikit (adopted)	H McDonald (USA)	1959
lace machine	J Leavers (UK)	1813
laser	T Maiman (USA)	1960
lightning conductor	B Franklin (USA)	1752
linotype machine	O Mergenthaler (USA)	1876–86
long-playing record (introduced)	P Goldmark (USA)	1948
loom, power	E Cartwright (UK)	1785
match	C Sauria (Fr)	1831
match, safety	J Lundstrom (Swe)	1855
magnetic recording	V Poulson (Den)	1898
margarine	H Mège-Mouries (Fr)	1863
nylon	W Carothers (USA)	1937
parking meter (first installed)	C Magee (USA)	1935
passenger lift	E Otis (USA)	1852
photographs, transmission by wireless	Sir W Stephenson (Can)	1922
piano	B Cristofori (It)	1720
postage stamp (introduced by)	R Hill (UK)	1840
radar	R Watson-Watt (UK)	1935
radio	G Marconi (It)	1896
rayon	Sir J Swan (UK)	1883
ribbed stocking machine	J Strutt (UK)	1735
rotary press	R Hoe (USA)	1846
rubber, latex foam	E Murphy (UK)	1928

Invention/Discovery	Name	Date
rubber, vulcanized	C Goodyear (USA)	1841
safety lamp	G Stephenson (UK)	1815
safety lamp, Davy	Sir H Davy (UK)	1816
safety pin	W Hunt (USA)	1849
safety razor	W Henson (UK)	1847
sewing machine (lockstitch)	W Hunt (USA)	1834
sextant	J Hadley (UK)	1730
Sheffield plate	T Boulsover (UK)	1742
spinning jenny	J Hargreaves (UK)	1760
spinning mule	S Crompton (UK)	1779
stocking frame	Rev. W Lee (UK)	1589
telegraph	W Coke and C Wheatstone (UK)	1876
telephone	Alexander G Bell (UK/USA)	1876
teleprinter	F Creed (Can)	1912
telescope	H Lippershay (Neth)	1608
television (first demonstrated)	J Baird (UK)	1926
terylene	J Dickson and J Whinfield (UK)	1941
torpedo	R Fulton (USA)	1805
transistor	W Shockley, J Bardeen and W Brattain (USA)	1947
zip fastener (patented)	W Jusdon (USA)	1891

Discoveries and Developments in Science

Discovery/Development	Name	Date
adrenalin	Takamin (Jap)	1901
anaesthesia	WTG Morton (USA), but earlier successes	1846
antiseptic surgery	J Lister (UK)	1867
aspirin	Dresser (Ger)	1889
atom, splitting of nucleus of	J D Cockcroft and ETS Walton (UK)	1932
atomic reactor (uranium fission)	E Fermi (It) and Szilard (USA)	1942
bleaching powder	S Tennant (UK)	1798
blood, circulation of	J Harvey (UK)	1628
Boyle's law	R Boyle (UK)	1662

Discovery/Development	Name	Date
chlorine	K W Scheele (Ger)	1774
chloroform	S Guthrie (USA)	1831
carbon-zinc cell	RW von Bunsen (Ger)	1841
cocaine	Niemann (Ger)	1860
cosmic rays	Gockel (Switz)	1910
cyanide	Caro (Ger)	1905
electric cell	RW von Bunsen (Ger)	1841
electromagnetic waves	J Clark Maxwell (UK)	1864
galvanic electricity	Galvani (It)	1762
germ theory of disease	L Pasteur (Fr)	1861
helium	Sir W Ramsay (UK)	1895
human heart transplant	C Barnard (SA)	1967
incubator (patented Champion 1770)	Drebbel (Neth)	1666
insulin	FG Banting, Best and Macleod	1922
magnesium	Sir H Davy (UK)	1808
motion, laws of	I Newton (UK)	1686
nitrogen	D Rutherford (UK)	1772
nitrous oxide (laughing gas)	Sir H Davy (UK)	1799
organic inheritance (genetics)	J Mendel (Aust)	1865–9
natural selection (*Origin of the Species*)	C Darwin (UK)	1859
oxygen	J Priestley (UK)	1774
quantum theory	M Planck (Ger)	1900
penicillin	Sir A Fleming (UK)	1929
penicillin, development of	Sir H Florey and EB Chain (UK)	1939
phosphorus	H Brand (Ger)	1669
plants, classification of	C Linnaeus (Swe)	1753
plutonium	GT Seaborg *et al* (USA)	1940
polio vaccine	J Salk (USA)	1954
radioactivity	AH Becquerel (Fr)	1896
radium	Curie, Pierre and Marie	1896
relativity, theory of	A Einstein (Ger/Switz)	1915 onwards
stethoscope	RT Laënnec	1819
streptomycin	DRS Waksman (USA)	1944
superphosphate	Sir JB Lawes (UK)	1842
thalium	Sir W Crookes (UK)	1861

Discovery/Development	Name	Date
thermometer	G Galilei (It)	1593
tubercle bacillus isolated	R Koch (Ger)	1822
uranium	MH Klaproth (Ger)	1789
vaccination	H Jenner (UK)	1796
Vitamin A	EV McCollum (USA)	1913
Vitamin B	EV McCollum (USA)	1916
Vitamin C	Host and Froelich (Nor)	1912
Vitamin D	EV McCollum (USA)	1922
X-rays	WK Röntgen (Ger)	1895

Developments in Transport

Early man travelled by land and by water, but it was a long time before there were any significant developments. On land people walked, travelled in carts, or rode horses. Eventually they built coaches and slowly these became more comfortable and elaborate; but they were still dependent on horses.

It was the same at sea. The first boats were paddled, and it was not until cloth was woven that men were able to utilise wind power. Boats became bigger, the rudder and the keel were invented; but man was still dependent on the wind.

It was the invention of the steam engine that transformed transport, and railways and cars were developed. Then, in a comparatively short time, man learned to fly.

Boats and Ships

Year BC Development

7,600   earliest surviving paddle (found in Yorkshire)

6,315   earliest surviving dug-out canoe (found in Pesse, Netherlands)

3,500   sails in use

2,515   earliest surviving boat (found buried near the Great Pyramid of Khufu (Cheops)

Year AD

280   floating fortress 182.8m^2 used in river war in China

1732   light-vessel stationed in the Thames estuary

1783   first boat propelled by steam, the paddle-steamer *Pyroscaphe* built in France

1789   first lifeboat, invented by Henry Greathead (patented by Lukin in 1785), stationed in the mouth of the R. Tyne

1792   Robert Fulton (USA) built the first submarine, *Nautilus*, in France

1801–2   *Charlotte Dundas*, first successful power-driven boat, designed by William Symington (UK)

1807   first paddle-steam ship, the *Clermont*, built by Robert Fulton in service on the R. Hudson

1812   *Comet* built by Henry Bell (UK)

1814–5   The *Fulton*, the first steam warship (38 tons) (USA)

1832   *Great Western*, designed by Isambard Kingdom Brunel (UK), first steamship to cross the Atlantic

1836   screw propeller designed by Sir Francis Pettit (UK)

1835   *Great Britain*, designed by Isambard Kingdom Brunel, first large steamship constructed of iron with screw propeller

1878   first oil tanker, built in Russia

1888   *Gymnote*, built in France, the first submersible torpedo boat

1894   *Turbinia*, the first turbine ship, designed by Sir Charles Parsons (UK)

1955   Sir Christopher Cockerell patented the hovercraft (UK)

1959   first flight of the Saunders-Roe SR-N1 hovercraft (UK)

1960   USS *Triton*, the first nuclear-powered submarine

1964   *Savannah* (USA) first nuclear-powered merchant ship

Road Transport

Year	Development
1769	steam-powered military tractor, designed by Nicholas-Joseph Cugnot (Fr), demonstrated in Paris, reached a speed of 3.6 km/h
1826	internal combustion engine with two-cylinder atmospheric engine built by Samuel Brown (UK)
1831	Cheltenham had the first steam-powered bus service (ran for four months)
1834	first mechanical reaper in service in the USA
1839–40	first bicycle constructed by Kirkpartrick MacMillan (UK)
1861	Etienne Lenoir (Fr) built a vehicle which used electrically ignited petroleum vapour
1874	first electric tram in service in the USA
1880	J B Dunlop (UK) invented the pneumatic tyre
1885	first petrol-driven three-wheeled car built by Karl-Friedrich Benz (Ger)
1885	first internal combustion wooden-framed motorized bicycle built by Gottlieb Daimler (Ger); capable of a top speed of 19 km/h
1888	Renault (Fr) built the first completely enclosed car
1903	first municipal bus service inaugurated in Eastbourne
1908	Model T Ford went into production
1915	*No 1 Lincoln*, the world's first tank designed by Sir Ernest Swinton (UK), tested; in service in the First World War in 1916
1979	rocket-engined Budweiser Rocket reached a speed of over 1190 km/h (USA)
1983	jet-engined Thrust 2 reached a speed of over 1,019 mph

Railways

Year	Development
1550	wagons hauled on wooden rails in Alsace, France
1758	first successful steam locomotive linked Middleton Colliery and Leeds (UK)
1804	Richard Trevithick's steam carriage ran on rails at a speed of 8 km/h (UK)
1825	first public service using steam traction, the Stockton and Darlington railway, opened; *Locomotion*, designed by George Stephenson reached 24 km/hr (UK)
1838	post-office van introduced on the London-Birmingham railway (UK)
1863	first underground railway opened in London (UK)
1869	first trans-continental railway completed in the USA
1879	demonstration of first practical electrical railway designed by Werner von Siemens (Ger)
1885	Canadian Pacific Railway completed
1905	Trans-Siberian railway completed (USSR)
1938	*Mallard*, reached a top speed of 203 km/h, a record that still stands for a steam locomotive (UK)
1981	BR ran its first Advanced Passenger Train service which reached a top speed of 644 km/h (UK)

Balloons, Airships and Aircraft

Year	Development
1783	Jacques and Etienne Montgolfier's (Fr) tethered balloon rose to about 305 m
1783	first flight in a hot-air balloon made by François de Rozer (Fr) who travelled about 8.5 km
1785	Jean-Pierre Blanchard (Fr) crossed the English Channel in a hydrogen-filled balloon
1852	Henri Giffard (Fr) made first flight in a steam-powered dirigible
1872	Paul Haenlein (Aust) flew first dirigible with an internal combustion engine
1903	Wilbur and Orville Wright (USA) made the first flight in their aircraft, the *Flyer*
1909	Louis Blériot (Fr) became the first man to fly an aircraft across the English Channel

Year	Development
1910	Eugene Ely (USA) became the first man to take off from a ship
1910	Henri Fabre (Fr) became the first man to take off from water in his monoplane floatplane
1914	HMS *Ark Royal*, the first aircraft carrier, launched
1919	first non-stop crossing of the Atlantic made by Alcock and Brown (USA)
1923	first in-flight refuelling
1926	first flight over North Pole, made by Richard Byrd (USA)
1926	Airship, the *Graf Zeppelin* made the first round-the-world flight
1927	first non-stop solo crossing of the Atlantic made by Charles Lindbergh (USA)
1929	first flight over the South Pole made by Richard Byrd (USA)
1933	first solo flight around the world made by Wiley Post in the *Winnie Mae*
1930	Amy Johnson made the first solo flight by a woman, from England to Australia
1932	Amelia Earhart (USA) made the first solo crossing of the Atlantic by a woman
1938	Boeing Model 307 Stratoliner became the first pressurized aircraft to enter passenger service
1944	the first jet aircraft, *Gloster Meteor Mark I*, entered service with the RAF
1947	Captain Charles Yeager made the first supersonic flight in a Bell XS-1 rocket plane (USA)
1949	Boeing-B50 Superfortress (USA) made the first non-stop flight round the world
1950	the Vickers Viscount V630 became the first turbine-powered aircraft to enter airline service
1976	Concorde (Fr & UK), the first supersonic aircraft, entered airline service
1980	*Solar Challenger* (USA) became the world's first solar-powered aircraft

Comparison of Time Taken to Go Round the World

Date	Craft	Time
1519–21	*Vittoria* (sailing ship)	2 years
1960	USS *Triton* (nuclear submarine)	2 months 25 days
1929	*Graf Zeppelin* (airship)	21 days 7 hr 34 mins
1924	*Chicago* (Douglas aircraft)	14 days 15 hours 11 mins
1957	USAF Boeing B–52 Superfortress	1 day 21 hrs 19 mins
1967	*Cosmos* 169 (satellite)	80 mins 30.6 secs

Chemical Elements

A chemical element is any substance consisting of atoms all having the same atomic number.

Element	Symbol	Atomic Number
Actinium	Ac	89
Aluminium	Al	13
Americium	Am	95
Antimony	Sb	51
Argon	Ar	18
Arsenic	As	33
Astatine	At	85
Barium	Ba	56
Berkelium	Bk	97
Beryllium	Be	4
Bismuth	Bi	83
Boron	B	5
Bromine	Br	35
Cadmium	Cd	48
Caesium	Cs	55
Calcium	Ca	20
Californium	Cf	98
Carbon	C	6
Chlorine	Cl	17

Element	Symbol	Atomic Number
Chromium	Cr	24
Cobalt	Co	27
Copper	Cu	29
Curium	Cm	96
Dysprosium	Dy	66
Einsteinium	Es	99
Erbium	Er	68
Europium	Eu	63
Fermium	Fm	100
Fluorine	F	9
Francium	Fr	87
Gadolinium	Gd	64
Gallium	Ga	31
Germanium	Ge	32
Gold	Au	79
Hafnium	Hf	72
Helium	He	2
Holmium	Ho	67
Hydrogen	H	1
Indium	In	49
Iodine	I	53
Iridium	Ir	77
Iron	Fe	26
Krypton	Kr	36
Lanthanum	La	57
Lawrencium	Lr	103
Lead	Pb	82
Lithium	Li	3
Lutetium	Lu	71
Magnesium	Mg	12
Manganese	Mn	25
Mendelevium	Md	101
Mercury	Hg	80
Molybdenum	Mo	42
Neodymium	Nd	60
Neon	Ne	10
Neptunium	Np	93
Nickel	Ni	28
Niobium	Nb	41

Element	Symbol	Atomic Number
Nitrogen	N	7
Nobelium	No	102
Osmium	Os	76
Oxygen	O	8
Palladium	Pd	46
Phosphorus	P	15
Platinum	Pt	78
Plutonium	Pu	94
Polonium	Po	84
Potassium	K	19
Praseodymium	Pr	59
Promethium	Pm	61
Protactinium	Pa	91
Radium	Ra	88
Radon	Rn	86
Rhenium	Re	75
Rhodium	Rh	45
Rubidium	Rb	37
Ruthenium	Ru	44
Samarium	Sm	62
Scandium	Sc	21
Selenium	Se	34
Silicon	Si	14
Silver	Ag	47
Sodium	Na	11
Strontium	Sr	38
Sulphur	S	16
Tantalum	Ta	73
Technetium	Tc	43
Tellurium	Te	52
Terbium	Tb	65
Thallium	Tl	81
Thorium	Th	90
Thulium	Tm	69
Tin	Sn	50
Titanium	Ti	22
Tungsten	W	74
Uranium	U	92
Vanadium	V	23

Element	Symbol	Atomic Number
Wolfran *see* Tungsten		
Xenon	Xe	54
Ytterbium	Yb	70
Yttrium	Y	39
Zinc	Zn	30
Zirconium	Zr	40

Relative Density (Specific Gravity)

Relative density is the ratio of the density of a substance to the density of a reference substance under specified conditions.

The relative density of gases is often measured with reference to air, both gases being at standard temperature and pressure.

Relative densities of solids and liquids are measured with reference to water, the density of the substance being taken at a specified temperature, usually 20°C, and the density of the water being taken at 4°C. Any substance with a relative density of less than 1 will float on water. If it is greater than 1, it will sink.

Relative Densities of Some Substances

Material	Relative Density
Cork	0.24
Oak	0.8
Water	1
Calcium	1.55
Aluminium	2.7
Diamond	3.5
Mercury	3.6
Titanium	4.5
Iodine	4.95
Arsenic	5.72
Tin	7.31
Steel	7.6–7.8
Silver	10.5
Gold	19.32
Platium	21.45

Some Familiar Substances

Common Name	Scientific Name
alum	potassium aluminium sulphate
antifreeze	ethylene glycol
aqua fortis	concentrated nitric acid
aqua regia	concentrated nitric and hydrochloric acids in the ratio of four to one
aspirin	acetylsalicylic acid
baking soda	sodium hydrogen carbonate
bleaching powder	chloride of lime
bromide	potassium bromide
calomel	mercurous chloride
carbolic acid	phenol
chalk	calcium carbonate
china clay (kaolin)	hydrated aluminium silicate
common salt	sodium chloride
cream of tartar	potassium hydrogen tartrate
Epsom salts	magnesium sulphate
gypsum	natural hydrated calcium sulphate
hypo	sodium thiosulphate
laughing gas	nitrous oxide
lime	calcium oxide
magnesia	magnesium oxide
nitre	potassium nitrate
oil of vitriol	concentrated sulphuric acid
oil of wintergreen	methyl salicylate
plaster of Paris	gypsum heated to 120°C–130°C; when mixed with water it hardens and sets
potash	potassium carbonate
prussic acid	hydrocyanic acid
quicksilver	mercury
sal volatile	ammonium carbonate
saltpetre	potassium nitrate
salts of lemon	potassium hydrogen oxalate
slaked lime	calcium hydroxide
spirits of salt	solution of hydrochloric acid
talc	hydrated magnesium silicate
TNT	trinitrotoluene
vaseline	petrolatum
vinegar	solution of acetic acid
washing soda	crystalline sodium carbonate

Gases

Name	Description
argon	colourless, odourless, tasteless, present in the atmosphere (0.94%), obtained as a by-product in the liquefaction of air; used in electric light bulbs, fluorescent tubes
butane	colourless with slight smell and taste, present in crude petroleum, used as a fuel when liquified in cylinders under pressure
carbon dioxide	colourless, almost odourless and tasteless, non-flammable, occurs in the atmosphere, the source of carbon for plants; used in carbonated drinks, fire extinguishers, as a refrigerant (dry ice) when solid
carbon monoxide	colourless, odourless, flammable, highly toxic gas when breathed; formed during the incomplete combustion of coke and similar fuels, burns with a blue flame; used as a fuel and as a reducing agent in metallurgy
chlorine	greenish-yellow with a strong smell, non-flammable poisonous gas occuring in many minerals; used to make paper, bleaching powder, hydrochloric acid, many organic compounds, used as a germicide in water
chloroethane	colourless with a burning taste, flammable, poisonous; used as a refrigerant, a local anaesthetic and an alkylating agent
coal-gas	produced by the destructive distillation of coal often supplemented with natural gas or water gas, composed of hydrogen, methane, carbon monoxide, other hydrocarbons and small amounts of nitrogen, carbon dioxide and oxygen; used as a fuel gas
helium	colourless, tasteless, odourless, very light, found in some natural gas, in radioactive ores, and in the atmosphere, also obtained as a by-product of the liquefaction of air; used in filling airships and balloons, and some fluorescent lamps

Name	Description
hydrogen	colourless, odourless, flammable, the lightest element in the universe, occurs in water in organic compounds and all living things, manufactured by a number of processes; used for the manufacture of synthetic ammonia and synthetic oil
hydrogen bromide	gas made by passing hydrogen and bromide vapour over a platinum catalyst
hydrogen chloride	gas made by reaction between concentrated sulphuric acid and sodium chloride
hydrogen iodide	gas made by passing hydrogen and iodine vapour over a platinum catalyst
hydrogen sulphide	the gas with the bad-egg smell, colourless, flammable, poisonous, made by the reaction of dilute acid to iron sulphide; used in metallurgy and chemical analysis
ketene	colourless, toxic, with strong smell; used in the manufacture of aspirin and cellulose acetate
krypton	colourless, odourless, tasteless, non-flammable gas present in the atmosphere, extracted as a by-product in the liquefaction of air; used in fluorescent lamps and some lasers
methane	marsh-gas or fire-damp, colourless, odourless, tasteless, flammable gas that forms an explosive mixture with air, occurs in coal gas and is the chief component in natural gas; used a fuel and a source of petrochemicals
methylamine	colourless, pungent, flammable, gaseous amine made by reacting methanol and ammonia at a very high temperature with a catalyst; used in the manufacture of dyes, insecticides and pharmaceuticals
mustard	colourless, oily liquid with a strong smell made by reacting ethylene with sulphur chloride; used as a war gas
natural	mixture of gaseous hydrocarbons, mainly methane, found beneath the surface of the earth and sea often near deposits of mineral oil; used as a fuel

Name	Description
neon	colourless, odourless, tasteless, non-flammable, present in the atmosphere in minute amounts, obtained as a by-product in the liquefaction of air; used in fluorescent lamps; a discharge of electricity through neon at low pressure produces a bright reddish-orange glow
nerve	attacks the nervous system, in particular those nerves controlling respiration; most of these gases are derived from phosphoric acid
nitrogen	colourless, odourless, tasteless, non-flammable, forms 78% of air by volume, obtained by the liquefaction of air; used in the manufacture of ammonia, nitric acid, and compounds such as fertilizers
nitrogen monoxide	colourless, non-flammable, poisonous, made by the oxidation of ammonia at tremendously high temperatures, reacts with air to give nitrogen dioxide
nitrous oxide	laughing gas, colourless, sweetish, non-flammable, made by heating ammonium nitrate; used as an anaesthetic
oxygen	colourless, tasteless, odourless, forms about 20% of the atmosphere by volume, the most abundant element in the earth's crust (49.2%), essential for the respiration of plants and animals, obtained by liquefying air; used in blast furnaces, welding, the manufacture of respirators and organic chemicals
phosgene	colourless, pungent, poisonous, made by passing carbon monoxide over activated carbon; used as a war gas and the manufacture of a number of organic chemicals
phosphine	colourless, pungent, spontaneously flammable, poisonous, made by dropping potassium hydroxide on phosphorus; used as a doping agent for semiconductors

Name	Description
producer	mixture of carbon monoxide and nitrogen made by passing air over hot coke, principal ingredients are carbon monoxide, nitrogen and hydrogen; used as a fuel
stibine	colourless, poisonous gas that decomposes to antimony and hydrogen on heating
xenon	colourless, odourless, tasteless, non-flammable, present in minute amounts in the atmosphere, extracted as a by-product in the liquefaction of air; used in light bulbs, fluorescent tubes, thermionic valves and some lasers.

Système International d'Unités (SI Units)

This system of units is used for all scientific purposes derived from the metre/kilogramme/second (MKS) system, and consisting of seven base and two supplementary units. Fifteen of these derived units have special names (*see* Table 2). Both base units and derived units with special names have agreed symbols. Decimal multiples and submultiples (*see* Table 3) in both base and derived units are expressed using standard prefixes.

Table 1: Base and Supplementary SI Units

Physical Quantity	SI Unit	Symbol for Unit
length	metre	m
mass	kilogramme	kg
time	second	s
electric current	ampere	A
thermodynamic temperature	kelvin	K
luminous intensity	candela	cd
amount of substance	mole	mol
★plain angle	radian	rad
★solid angle	steradian	sr
★supplementary units		

Table 2: Derived SI Units with Special Names

Physical Quantity	SI Unit	Symbol for Unit
frequency	hertz	Hz
energy	joule	J
force	newton	N
power	watt	W
pressure	pascal	Pa
electric charge	coulomb	C
electric potential difference	volt	V
electric resistance	ohm	Ω
electric conductance	siemens	S
electric capacitance	farad	F
magnetic flux	weber	Wb
inductance	henry	H
magnetic flux density (magnetic induction)	tesla	T
luminous flux	lumen	lm
illuminance (illumination)	lux	lx

Table 3: Decimal Multiples and Submultiples to be used with SI Units

submultiple	prefix	symbol	multiple	prefix	symbol
10^{-1}	deci	d	10^{1}	deca	da
10^{-2}	centi	c	10^{2}	hecto	h
10^{-3}	milli	m	10^{3}	kilo	k
10^{-6}	micro	μ	10^{6}	mega	M
10^{-9}	nano	n	10^{9}	giga	G
10^{-12}	pico	p	10^{10}	tera	T
10^{-15}	femto	f			
10^{-18}	atto	a			

Note: all symbols should be used without full stops

Fundamental Constants

velocity of light	c	$2.997\,925 \times 10^8$	$m\,s^{-1}$
magnetic constant	μ_o	$1.256\,64 \times 10^{-6}$	$H\,m^{-1}$
electric constant	ε_o	$8.854\,16 \times 10^{-12}$	$F\,m^{-1}$
electron charge	e	$1.602\,192 \times 10^{-19}$	C
electron mass	m_c	$9.109\,558 \times 10^{-31}$	kg
proton mass	m_p	$1.672\,614 \times 10^{-27}$	kg
Avogadro constant	N	$6.022\,52 \times 10^{23}$	mol^{-1}
Bolzmann constant	k	$1.380\,622 \times^{-23}$	$J\,K^{-1}$
Planck constant	h	$6.626\,196 \times 10^{-34}$	$J\,s$
Lockschmidt's number	L	$2.687\,19 \times 10^{25}$	m^{-3}
Faraday constant	F	$9.648\,670 \times 10^4$	$C\,mol^{-1}$
gas constant	R	$8.314\,34$	$J\,K^{-1}\,mol^{-1}$
standard acceleration of free fall	g	$9.806\,65$	$m\,s^{-2}$
standard atmospheric pressure	p	$1.013\,25 \times 10^5$	Pa

Mohs' Scale

This scale is designed to indicate the hardness of minerals. Talc, the softest, is given the number of 1 on the scale, and a diamond, the hardest, is assigned the number 10. Each mineral is capable of scratching any other mineral that is lower on the scale.

1 talc	5 apatite	8 topaz
2 gypsum	6 orthoclase	9 corundum
3 calcite	7 quartz	10 diamond
4 fluorite		

Numbers

We use Arabic numerals which run from 0–9. They were invented round about AD 520 by Indians who also had a decimal system. The Arabs adopted them in AD 760, and developed algebra and trigonometry.

Arabic Numerals	Roman Numerals	Cardinal Numbers
1	I	1st (first)
2	II	2nd (second)
3	III	3rd (third)
4	IV	4th (fourth)
5	V	5th (fifth)
6	VI	6th (sixth)
7	VII	7th (seventh)
8	VIII	8th (eighth)
9	IX	9th (ninth)
10	X	10th (tenth)
50	L	50th (fiftieth)
100	C	100th (hundredth)
500	D	500th (five hundredth)
1,000	M	1,000th (thousandth)

Conversion of Roman Numerals to Arabic Numerals

When a larger numeral precedes a smaller numeral, add the smaller numeral to the larger:

$$XV = X + V = 10 + 5 = 15$$
$$LXI = L + X + I = 50 + 10 + 1 = 51$$

When a smaller numeral precedes a larger numeral, subtract it from the numeral that follows it:

$$XIX = X + (X - I) = 10 + (10 - 1) = 19$$
$$MMDCIV = M + M + D + C + (V - I) = 1,000 + 1,000 + 500 + 100 + (5 - 1) = 2,604$$

Metric Measurement

Linear Measurement

10 millimetres	= 1 centimetre	= 0.3937 inches
10 centimetres	= 1 decimetre	= 3.937 inches
10 decimetres	= 1 metre	= 39.37 inches (3.28 feet)
10 metres	= 1 decametre	= 393.7 inches (32.8 feet)
10 decametres	= 1 hectometre	= 328 feet 1 inch

Linear Measurement

10 hectometres = 1 kilometre   = 0.6214 mile (1,093.6 yards)
10 kilometres   = 1 myriametre = 6.214 miles

Square Measurement

100 sq. millimetres = 1 sq. centimetre = 0.15499 sq. inches
100 sq. centimetres = 1 sq. decimetre = 15.499 sq. inches
100 sq. decimetres   = 1 sq. metre   = 1,549.9 sq. inches
100 sq. metres   = 1 sq. decametre = 119.6 sq. yards
100 sq. decametres   = 1 sq. hectometre = 2.471 acres
100 sq. hectometres = 1 sq. kilometre = 0.386 sq. mile

Land Measurement

1 sq. metre   = 1 centiare   = 1,549.9 sq. inches
10 centiares = 1 are   = 119.6 sq. yards
100 ares   = 1 hectare   = 2.471 acres
100 hectares = 1 sq. kilometre = 0.386 sq. mile

Cubic Measurement

1,000 cubic millimetres = 1 cubic centimetre = 0.0610 cubic inches
1,000 cubic centimetres = 1 cubic decimetre = 61.024 cubic inches
1,000 cubic decimetres   = 1 cubic metre   = 35.3146 cubic feet

Volume Measurement

1,000 cubic millimetres = 1 cubic centimetre = 0.0610 cubic inches
1,000 cubic centimetres = 1 cubic decimetre = 61.02 cubic inches
1,000 cubic decimetres   = 1 cubic metre   = 35.314 cubic feet

Capacity Measurement

10 millilitres = 1 centilitre = 0.338 fluid ounces
10 centilitres = 1 decilitre   = 3.38 fluid ounces
10 decilitres   = 1 litre   = 1.0567 liquid quarts
                                     (0.9081 dry quarts)
10 litres   = 1 decalitre   = 2.64 gallons (0.284 bushels)
10 decalitres   = 1 hectolitre = 26.418 gallons (2.838 bushels)
10 hectolitres = 1 kilolitre   = 264.18 gallons (35.315)

Weight

10 milligrammes	= 1 centigramme	= 0.1543 grains
10 centigrammes	= 1 decigramme	= 1.5432 grains
10 decigrammes	= 1 gramme	= 15.432 grains
10 grammes	= 1 decagramme	= 0.3527 ounces
10 decagrammes	= 1 hectogramme	= 3.3527 ounces
10 hectogrammes	= 1 kilogramme	= 2.2046 pounds
10 kilogrammes	= 1 myriagramme	= 22.046 pounds
10 myriagrammes	= 1 quintal	= 220.46 pounds
10 quintals	= 1 metric ton	= 2204.6 pounds

Angular Measurement

60 seconds	= 1 minute
60 minutes	= 1 degree
90 degrees	= 1 quadrant (right angle)
4 quadrants	= 1 circle = 360 degrees

Imperial Measurement

Linear Measurement

1 inch	=		0.0254 m
1 foot	=	12 inches	= 0.3048 m
1 yard	=	3 feet	= 0.9144 m
22 yards	=	1 chain	
10 chains	=	1 furlong	
8 furlongs	=	1 mile	= 1,609.34 m
		1,760 yards	
3 miles	=	1 (land league)	= 4.83 m
Note:		1.09361 yards	= 1.0 m
		0.621371 miles	= 1.0 km

Square Measurement

1 square inch			= 6.452 cm^2
144 square inches	=	1 square foot	= 929 cm^2
9 square feet	=	1 square yard	= 0.8361 m^2
4,840 square yards	=	1 acre	= 0.4047 hectares
640 acres	=	1 square mile	= 2.59 km^2

Cubic Measurement

1 cubic inch			=	16.387 cm^3
1,728 cubic inches	=	1 cubic foot	=	0.0283 m^3
27 cubic feet	=	1 cubic yard	=	0.7646 m^3

Volume Measurement

1 minim	=	1/9600 pint		
60 minims	=	1 fluid drachm		
8 fluid drachms	=	1 fluid ounce	=	0.0296 litre
5 fluid ounces	=	1 gill		
4 gills	=	1 pint	=	0.4732 litre
2 pints	=	1 quart	=	0.9463 litre
4 quarts	=	1 gallon	=	3.7853 litres

Note: 1 gallon (USA) = 0.832628 gallon (UK)

Avoirdupois Units of Mass

1 grain	=	1/700 pound	=	0.064799 g
1 dram	=	1/256 pound		
16 drams	=	1 ounce	=	113.398 g
16 ounces	=	1 pound	=	0.453592 g
14 pounds	=	1 stone		
2 stones	=	1 quarter		
4 quarters	=	1 hundredweight	=	50.802 kg
	=	112 pounds		
20 hundredweights	=	1 ton	=	1016.047 kg
	=	2240 pounds		

Note: avoirdupois hundredweight is sometimes called the long hundredweight; avoirdupois ton is sometimes called the long ton. This is to distinguish them from the US measure in which the short hundredweight = 100 pounds, the short ton = 2,000 pounds

Troy Units of Mass

Troy weight is a system devised for use with precious stones and precious metals

1 grain	=	1/700 pound
4 grains	=	1 carat
6 carats	=	1 pennyweight
20 pennyweights	=	1 ounce
12 ounces	=	1 pound
100 pounds	=	1 hundredweight
20 hundredweights	=	1 ton

Apothecaries' Units of Mass

1 grain	=	1/700 pound (avoirdupois)
20 grains	=	1 scruple
3 scruples	=	1 drachm
8 drachms	=	1 ounce (apoth)
12 ounces (apoth)	=	1 pound (apoth)

Mass: Conversion Factors

The unit of mass is the kilogramme.

	kg	g	pound (lb)	*ton (long)
1 kilogramme	1	1000	2.20462	9.84207×10^{-4}
1 gramme	10^{-3}	1	2.20462×10^{-3}	9.84207×10^{-7}
1 pound	0.453592	453.592	1	4.46429×10^{-4}
1 long ton	1016.047	1.016047×10^6	2240	1

*see Avoirdupois Units of Mass

Velocity: Conversion Factors

Velocity is measured in metres per second.

	m/sec	km/hr	mile/hour	ft/sec
1 metre per second	1	3.6	2.23694	3.28084
1 kilometre per hour	0.277778	1	0.621371	0.911346
1 mile per hour	0.44704	1.609344	1	1.46667
1 foot per second	0.3048	1.09728	0.681817	1

Conversion of mph to km/hr

mph	km/hr
1	1.609344
5	8.04627
10	16.09344
15	24.14016
20	32.18688
25	40.23360
30	48.28032
35	56.32704
40	64.37376
45	72.42048
50	80.46720
55	88.51392
60	96.56064
65	104.60736
70	112.65408
75	120.70080
80	128.74752
85	136.79424
90	144.84098
95	152.88768
100	160.93440

Conversion of km/hr to mph

km/hr	mph
1	0.621371
5	3.106855
10	6.213710
15	9.320565
20	12.427420
25	15.534275
30	18.641130
35	21.747985
40	24.854840
45	27.961695
50	31.068550
55	34.175405
60	37.282260
65	40.389115
70	43.495970
75	46.602825
80	49.709560
85	52.816535
90	55.923390
95	59.030245
100	62.137100

Nautical Measurement

A nautical mile is a linear measurement for ships and aircraft.

6 feet	= 1 fathom
1 nautical mile (international)	= 1.1508 statue miles (the length of a minute of longitude at the equator)
3 nautical miles	= 1 marine league (3.45 statute miles or 5.56 kilometres)
60 nautical miles	= 1 degree

Note: 1 knot = 1 nautical mile per hour

International Paper Sizes

A0 = 841 × 1,189 millimetres
A1 = 594 ×   841 millimetres
A2 = 420 ×   594 millimetres
A3 = 297 ×   420 millimetres
A4 = 210 ×   297 millimetres
A5 = 148 ×   210 millimetres
A6 = 105 ×   148 millimetres
A7 =   74 ×   105 millimetres
A8 =   52 ×   72 millimetres
A9 =   37 ×   52 millimetres
A10 =   26 ×   37 millimetres

Mathematical Signs

+ plus, the sign of addition; sometimes used to indicate that figures are only approximately exact since some figures have been omitted from the end, e.g., 4.1096 +

− minus, the sign of subtraction; sometimes used to indicate that figures have been omitted from the end of a number and that the last figure has been increased by one, e.g., 9.2378 = 9.24−

× multiplied by, e.g., 6 × 4 = 24; also indicated by a centred dot, e.g., 6 · 4 = 24

÷ divided by; also indicated by a straight line between the divisor and the dividend, e.g., $\frac{a}{b}$ or by an oblique line, e.g., a/b

= is equal to; equals

≠ is not equal to

> is greater than, e.g., x > y, i.e., x is greater than y

< is less than, e.g., a < b, i.e., a is less than b

: as, equals; the ratio of

∴ therefore

∵ since, because

∠ angle, e.g., ∠ ABC

∟ right angle

⊥ the perpendicular, is perpendicular to, e.g., AB ⊥ CD

° degree, e.g., 90°

′ minute of an arc

″ seconds of an arc

Mathematical Formulae to Find Area

Circle: Multiply the square of the diameter by .7854
Rectangle: Multiply the length of the base by the height
Square: Square the length of one side
Triangle: Multiply the base by the perpendicular height and
             divide by 2

Conversion of Centigrade and Fahrenheit Temperatures

Anders Celcius (1701–44) invented the centigrade thermometer with a boiling point at 100° and a freezing point at 0°.

Gabriel Fahrenheit (1688–1736) introduced the fahrenheit scale with a boiling point at 212° and a freezing point at 32°F.

Conversion of Centigrade into Fahrenheit: multiply by 9, divide by 5, add 32. Conversion of Fahrenheit into Centigrade: subtract 32, multiply by 5, divide by 9.

Polygons and Polyhedrons

Polygons

A polygon is any plane figure bounded by straight lines.

Number of Lines	Name	Number of Lines	Name
3	triangle	7	septagon
4	rectangle	8	octagon
5	pentagon	10	decagon
6	hexagon	12	dodecagon

Polyhedrons

A polyhedron is an solid figure with polygons as its faces. Regular polyhedrons are those with all faces of the same shape and size.

Number of Faces	Name
4 triangular faces	tetrahedron
6 square faces	cube
8 triangular faces	octahedron
12 five-sided faces	dodecahedron
20 triangular faces	icosahedron